OWNING GRIEF

OWNING GRIEF

WIDOWED YOUNG, HOW I DISCOVERED GIFTS IN LOSS

GAEL GARBARINO CULLEN

Linda,
Own it!
Gael Garbarino Cullen

iUniverse®

OWNING GRIEF
WIDOWED YOUNG, HOW I DISCOVERED GIFTS IN LOSS

iUniverse books may be ordered through booksellers or by contacting:

iUniverse
1663 Liberty Drive
Bloomington, IN 47403
www.iuniverse.com
844-349-9409

Cover art designed and illustrated by Aaron Johnson

ISBN: 978-1-6632-4351-5 (sc)
ISBN: 978-1-6632-4352-2 (e)

Library of Congress Control Number: 2022914161

Print information available on the last page.

iUniverse rev. date: 08/23/2022

CONTENTS

DEDICATION

To Steve, for the consummate gift of our four children. Annie, Kathleen, Molly and Colleen challenge and inspire me in everything that I do. For each of them I am blessed beyond measure.

FOREWORD

They were Milwaukee's most appealing power couple – a spirited, strapping city alderman and his wife, the charming, award-winning TV reporter. You could easily imagine them in Washington, D.C. someday with their four darling daughters, capturing the nation's fancy.

When Steve Cullen died suddenly in October of 1995, shockwaves rippled across the newsroom of the *Milwaukee Journal Sentinel* where I worked as a reporter. How could this booming force of nature fall silent so suddenly? How will Gael, now a widow at forty-one, manage to raise these little girls alone? With my own young kids at home, I couldn't help but wonder how I might cope, if, God forbid, that same terrible hand should be dealt to me.

Days later, crammed into St. Catherine's Catholic Church in Milwaukee with more than 1,000 other mourners, I sat in a back pew, watching in awe as Gael stood up at the end of the funeral and strided toward the podium. She sized up the crowd with determined eyes, took a deep breath and declared to us all how much she loved Steve and always would. She would make sure that her girls would never forget him. I could see shoulders shaking and hear the muffled sounds of sobbing, including my own, at her powerful, heartbreaking testimony. We all stumbled out of church in a kind of daze.

Gael and I met up again about six years later when our two oldest children joined the Ulster Project, a collaborative to get Catholic and Protestant teenagers from America and Northern Ireland together. Noble as its mission was, the reality was four weeks of nearly nonstop schlepping from water parks to concerts to pool parties. From what I could see, Gael was bravely soldiering on. True to her word, she was somehow managing to raise these girls on her own, working to make ends meet, cooking, cleaning, shoveling, raking, and driving – lots and lots and lots of driving.

Having lost a sister and brother to suicide, I knew more than I wanted to about grief. People often ask how you can keep going in the face of such tragedy, when the simple truth is, you don't have any other good choices. This was especially true for Gael. She and I spent several hours together that summer having soulful discussions about this. I could see right away that Gael was the kind of person you'd want to spend time with. She does not shy away from talking about the tough stuff, but, at the same time, there is no bitterness to her. She has that winning combination of being tough-minded and tender-hearted. With each conversation we had, I found new reasons to admire her.

Though Gael and I did not see one another often, our lives kept crisscrossing. I always look forward to seeing her. When I learned that she was writing a memoir, I was intrigued. How indeed had she managed all these years? She sent me a copy of her latest draft. I told myself that I'd read a few chapters and get to the rest when I could. I'm finishing my own memoir and was busy teaching investigative reporting at Columbia University's Graduate School of Journalism. To top it off, I'd just had hip replacement surgery and was battling Covid, alone in New York City.

After the first chapter, I knew I could not let go. By 2:30 a.m. I'd finished the whole book, bleary-eyed but eager to go back and read it again. There is so much wisdom here, compelling lessons for anyone who has suffered an unexpected loss or found themselves alone with crushing responsibilities.

I can only imagine how painful this was for her to write, revisiting those terrifying hours as she desperately searched for answers to why Steve had not made it home from a business trip to Cincinnati. Or, the agonizing days leading up to his funeral, or the months and years that followed, watching her girls struggle, another Father's Day with no father to celebrate. And, yet, this is a book of hope and triumph. There is so much to celebrate.

Even if you never met Steve, you will know this fun-loving man once you have read this book. Gael, a skilled journalist, brings Steve's spirit back to life with her words. Readers will sit with Gael as she pours over bills, worrying about how she will keep her girls in their childhood home. You will stand at her side in exhaustion and despair as she shovels her driveway late one winter night. You will delight as her girls grow to become strong, determined women like their mother. You will imagine the pride that Steve would feel if he could see how this all turned out.

Gael has given us all a great gift with this book, the unblinking account of how she found the strength to keep going, because she had to.

Just as her words in church that October morning gave us all reason to believe she would find a way to make this work, this strong, brave woman's book will help others through their grief and confusion and fear. Gael has shown us how to do so with grace, humor and a tender heart.

Meg Kissinger
Columbia University Graduate School of Journalism
Pulitzer Prize Finalist

INTRODUCTION

"I don't know how you did it. I don't think I ever could have done what you've done."

That's the common refrain when people hear that I was widowed at forty-one, suddenly left to raise four small daughters totally on my own.

To this day my response is always the same: "When you don't have a choice, you figure it out."

I had daughters, ages nine, eight, five, and three. Their lives were just beginning. I owed it to them, and to me, to find a way to work through unspeakable grief and a frightening lost sense of security, to find happiness, joy, and the ability to hope again. It was a daunting challenge, to be sure. Daunting enough when your life's partner is by your side to help navigate the often choppy waters of childhood, adolescence, and the teen years. Downright terrifying to have to deal with science projects, orthodontia, father-daughter dances, first romances, college entrance exams, and myriad more life markers completely alone.

They don't have courses that teach you how to be a good parent. Most of us find ourselves ill-prepared for this most important of jobs, but with another parent to lean on, to consult with, to dream with, we tend to figure it out. But single parenthood, not by choice but by a sudden cardiac arrhythmia that stripped the life out of a seemingly healthy young dad, was uncharted, unwanted, unthinkable territory.

As a news reporter who daily was handed complicated subject matter with the assignment of figuring out the story quickly and relating it in a way that was easily understood, I'd always prided myself on being resourceful, a quick study. The city council's 90-page budget proposal? Been there, done that. A new breakthrough medical procedure? No problem. A presidential debate on foreign policy? Now that sounds like fun! Throw a challenge my way and I was on it. But suddenly single motherhood? There were no easy answers. No cache of inspirational wisdom to tap into. No way to Google the best way to handle the litany of issues, worries, heartbreaks, and life lessons that lie ahead for me or my girls. Nor to single-handedly take on the monumental task of molding these four babies into smart, socially conscious, successful women.

This book describes my experience and growth as a young mother in the web of grief and single parenthood. It speaks to my discovery of determination and resiliency, two attributes that have played and continue to play an essential role in my life's journey, as a parent, a careerwoman, and as a human being. In no way does this book suggest a prescription for success on the rocky path of death and loss. But perhaps the pages that follow will offer some hope that with love, tears, courage, friendship, and a healthy dose of laughter, it is possible to own your grief and maybe even discover some unexpected gifts along the way.

As first-time parents, Steve and I were on top of the world, sharing all the hopes and dreams and trepidation that comes with the job.

CHAPTER ONE

THE JOURNEY BEGINS

"On the other side of a storm is the strength that comes from having navigated through it. Raise your sail and begin."

Gregory S. Williams, author

"Tell me where my husband is!"

Uncertainty, fear, and sheer terror all fused into that strangled shriek into the phone receiver. And at the very moment those desperate, panicked words rose from my gut into my mouth, I faced another, equally terrifying realization. My nine-year-old, tucked safely into bed twenty minutes earlier as I bravely tried to pretend it was just another ordinary school night, had somehow known better. Something was not right. She had made her way downstairs to the kitchen just in time to witness the near collapse of her mother, of their world.

It was October 12, 1995. My forty-year-old husband, Steve, had left for a business trip to Cincinnati four days earlier and was supposed to return home to Milwaukee that day. The plan was that I would collect our three older girls, ages nine, eight, and five from their schools after work. Steve would pick up our three-year-old from the babysitter and we'd meet at home for dinner. Or so I thought.

I didn't recall the exact details of Steve's flight or airline. He traveled enough for business that a general understanding of when and where to expect him had always seemed sufficient. So when the babysitter called me at 4pm to say that Steve had not yet picked up Colleen, I was mildly annoyed, but not alarmed. I apologized to the sitter, "I'll be right there."

The typical after-school crush ensued. Between all the "how was school today" small talk and necessary help with homework, I managed to cook dinner and serve it up to our hungry brood. I still hadn't heard from Steve, but I was sure his flight must have been delayed and he had no easy access to a phone. Certainly he was now airborne.

5:30pm. The dishes were cleaned up followed by more quizzing for tomorrow's spelling test and this week's arithmetic problems. Occasionally one of the girls would remark, "I thought Daddy was coming home today," only to be reassured that he was just delayed. Nothing to worry about.

By 6 o'clock, what had seemed to be just a question of crossed signals or a possible airline issue was now beginning to gnaw at me. Steve always called every day when he was out of town on business, a bit of a challenge in the mid-90s when cell phones were not in everyone's pocket. He hadn't called the night before. That was odd, but I had dismissed it, figuring the closing dinner at his conference must have gone long and he didn't want to call too late. But surely if he knew his flight was being changed or re-routed wouldn't he have somehow left me a message?

6:45pm. With each passing moment, I tried to concentrate on the girls and not let on that I was in any way concerned.

There was the distraction of baths, goodnight stories, and prayers. Yet with each sweep of the minute hand, I grew more anxious. More anxious to get the girls tucked safely into bed upstairs so that I could begin to make phone calls from the kitchen, where they wouldn't hear me, to find out what had happened, why Steve wasn't home.

Now 7pm. The bedtime ritual complete, I forced myself to wait ten more long minutes so that the girls would settle in and, I hoped, fall asleep. Then began a chain of feverish phone calls. First to the airline. "No, the flight was on time, ma'am, but no Steve Cullen ever boarded it." And he hadn't boarded the following flight to Milwaukee either. To a colleague who had traveled with Steve on the business trip, who said, "I assumed Steve must have re-booked to get an earlier flight home." To the hotel in Cincinnati where I was bounced from a front desk attendant to the manager who put me on hold for agonizing minutes. When the manager finally returned to the phone with "we can't tell you anything, ma'am. You'll need to call Cincinnati police," all of my suppressed fears erupted as I demanded an answer, frozen in an inability to endure one more phone call.

"Tell me where my husband is!"

What followed was a short, agonized description of how housekeeping had gone to clean Steve's locked hotel room only to discover him dead in bed. No signs of trauma. Steve had apparently gone to sleep and never awoken. Cincinnati police might be able to provide additional details, I was told, including the likely need for an autopsy, which is standard procedure for any sudden, unexplained death. There may have been more but I couldn't hear it, couldn't process it. What I did hear was a small, terrorized voice, "Mom. What's wrong?" And for the first time I realized that my nine-year-old Annie had been standing in the kitchen doorway, for

3

how long I didn't know, witnessing my increasingly frantic phone conversations.

Soon the other girls were awake, too. An onslaught of despair gripped us all...screams... disbelief...an inability to catch our breath. There were phone calls. To my brother-in-law who answered that my sister, my rock, Joan, wasn't home. To Steve's mom. Probably to others, but in the shroud of shock that was fast settling in, the precise details are a blur.

What I do recall is the house filling up quickly with family and friends each unable to process the news of Steve's death. He was just forty-years-old. He had run a marathon, 26.2 miles, the day he left for Cincinnati. He was healthy. He was active.

None of it made sense. Not for me, suddenly a widow at forty-one, stripped of the man who was supposed to grow old beside her. Not for our kids, just babies really with full lives to build without their foundation, their Daddy. With our world suddenly, viciously ripped apart, we had to figure out how to glue it back together, a task, a journey none of us could have imagined.

Steve on his final business trip to Cincinnati
three days before he died.

CHAPTER TWO

LIFE AS WE KNEW IT

"Your story is what you have, what you will always have. It is something to own."

Michelle Obama, Former First Lady

"Are you doing anything Friday night?" It wasn't exactly a pickup line for the ages, but considering it was delivered in the small lunchroom at work with a host of curious ears and eyes not so subtly paying attention, it worked in the moment.

I was doing public relations for the Milwaukee Common Council, my first career job fresh out of college. In a new city where I hadn't yet had time to make many new friends, Steve Cullen, a handsome, outgoing assistant to one of the aldermen had caught my eye. But the few short encounters we'd had over the Xerox machine or the coffeemaker had not seemed to offer any hope of more than casual conversation.

And then, somewhat out of the blue, came this.

"I've got tickets to a musical Friday and I was wondering if you'd like to go with me?"

The sudden, unexpected nature of this request was

telling. You see, Steve and I first started dating quite by accident. Perhaps it was in some way an odd foreshadowing; one curious set of circumstances that brought us together, followed seventeen years later by a tragic new circumstance that would rip us apart.

I was fresh out of college. A naïve, ambitious twenty-two, I was hoping to ply my freshly minted journalism degree into a radio or TV news reporter job pretty much anywhere in the Midwest. The thought of exercising my new independence, but not too far from my Detroit roots and large family, was intriguing. My eldest sister, Joan, had settled in Milwaukee and encouraged me to consider Wisconsin. I have to admit I liked the idea of having at least one family tie waiting for me as I headed off into the unknown in my 1969 VW bug, rusted floor boards and all, so Milwaukee quickly became a solid prospect for launching my career.

I managed to land a very part-time reporting gig at a Milwaukee all-news radio station, but I needed something more substantial to pay the bills so I could move out of my sister's spare bedroom and into my own apartment. Public relations seemed an acceptable second-cousin-once-removed from journalism, so when a full-time PR job opened up with the city of Milwaukee's governing body, the Common Council, I swallowed my pride and opted for financial stability.

The Common Council press secretary, my boss, situated me at the end of a line of desks for administrative assistants, secretaries in the non-PC lingo of the time, each assigned to an individual alderman or Council member. Curiously, one of these assistants was another Gail who, unlike me, spelled her name the traditional way.

Steve was finishing his last semester in college, majoring in political science, so his work as an intern for one of Milwaukee's aldermen was a natural fit. He had recently broken up with his high school girlfriend and found himself suddenly dateless for an upcoming outdoor music theater's production of "1776" in honor of the United States Bicentennial. When young, charismatic Steve turned to the bank of administrative assistants for advice with his dating dilemma, someone suggested "Why not ask Gael?"

Steve immediately assumed it was Gail with an "i" and he wondered if she might be a bit too old for him. "No, not that Gail, he was told. "Gael Garbarino." Steve had thought I was married because of my young nephew's baby photo on my desk. Once corrected, he quickly decided Gael with an "e" was a good suggestion and our accidental first date took place that Friday.

Steve was an attractive, politically ambitious guy with a dry, sarcastic wit, which I loved. Unlike my own tendencies to tuck feelings inside and avoid confrontation at all costs, Steve was never afraid to say exactly what he thought. He stood by his principles, often at political risk, and he refused to tell anyone what they wanted to hear if he disagreed with them. He was boldly honest. Ironically, this characteristic that I so admired also had a dark side.

Steve's brash attitude often came across as cocky, especially coming from someone just barely into his twenties. Many a time, feelings were hurt, including my own, when Steve would insist that his way was the only way. That no one else's opinion mattered. Tact was not in young Steve's wheelhouse and the lack of it nearly cost us our marriage.

Living in different states, my mom had met Steve for the first time shortly after we announced our plans to be married. I thought a weekend in Detroit to meet my family would be a good exercise for all involved. It turned out to be awkward at best.

My mom, whom we lovingly referred to as Muzzie, was

a pretty opinionated person about life in general, politics, religion, and social issues. On that, she and Steve were very much alike. Unfortunately, their specific opinions tended to run polar opposite of each other for the most part. Steve was a progressive Democrat. Muzzie was a Nixon supporter. Steve was a casual Methodist. My mom was a card-carrying, no-way-but-the-pope's-way Catholic. For a woman who'd gone to work fresh out of high school to help support her family during the Depression, the concept of government "handouts" ran counter to everything she knew. Yet Steve insisted there was a legitimate role for the government to play in the lives of the less fortunate.

When the conversation started to turn to a subject, any subject that I feared might provoke an argument during our meet-the-family weekend, I tried to play the mediator, but to little avail. This put me in an exceedingly uncomfortable position, caught between two people I loved so dearly.

"Why can't you just keep your opinions to yourself for once," I hissed at Steve. "It doesn't do any good to make her mad."

We managed to escape back to Wisconsin without any blood being shed, but my mother, not one to let someone else have the last word, soon announced she was coming for a visit. It was rare for her to book a plane ticket to Milwaukee without some momentous family celebration to draw her there, so I was a little nervous. For good reason.

Within moments of the dinner dishes being cleared away, my mom insisted we all take a seat in the living room.

"I don't think the two of you should get married," she began, not wasting any time. "I think you deserve better, Gael, someone who respects you."

Clearly she took this young upstart's willingness to go toe-to-toe with her as a sign of disrespect for others in general, and her mama bear instincts were to protect her daughter from that fate. Her words, her message, cut both Steve and me to the core, but in a rare moment of bravery, I stood up to my mother and defended the man I loved.

"You're wrong, Mom," I remember stating as I wiped away my tears, holding fast onto Steve's hand. "Steve and I love each other and respect each other, and we want to spend the rest of our lives together."

For his part, Steve too, tried to assure my mother that we were insanely happy and that we looked forward to raising a family together, but when my mom remained unmoved, I decided to end the conversation.

"I am heartbroken that you don't want to believe us, Mom," I said. "If that means that you won't attend our wedding, that will crush me, but it won't stop me. Steve and I are getting married whether you're there or not."

What my mom didn't see then, but eventually came to appreciate, was that Steve was a complex guy, certainly with his share of flaws, but also with a great many admirable qualities. This was a man who played Santa at a central city shopping mall every year at Christmas time, giving up nights and weekends after working his day job to help spread the magic of the season to underprivileged children. In his early twenties without the girth or beard of his own to pull off the role, Steve happily stuffed pillows into his red suit and applied white facial hair and a wig night after night, delighting in this spare job perhaps as much as the kids whose deepest Christmas secrets he shared.

We were pretty smitten with each other from the start. We shared a love of baseball and college football. Of social consciousness and good friends, and anything Milwaukee. Of rock and roll music and outdoor concerts. Of playing poker or board games with friends. Of big families. Brothers and sisters abounded between us and we soon vowed that the large family tradition would continue with us. Two years after that first date, we were married and our life together took off. Another two years later Steve put his political chops to the test and was elected one of the youngest ever to win an Aldermanic campaign in Milwaukee, a seat he held for twelve years.

My journalistic ambitions were also paying dividends. No longer a radio news anchor at WBCS "Big Country Sound," sister-station to the now-defunct all-news station where I began my career, I had landed a morning news anchor spot at the flagship Milwaukee station, WTMJ-AM. The beauty of this move was that it put me literally steps closer to the TV news slot I longed for, as WTMJ-AM shared the same newsroom with WTMJ-TV, the local NBC affiliate. I volunteered for any TV news story that no one else wanted and made sure to seek out big brotherly advice from the TV assignment editor. When a full-time TV reporter spot opened up, I had sufficiently proven myself, perhaps ingratiated myself, to the point where I was the natural choice in a highly competitive market.

The big family we envisioned turned out to be a bit more challenging than fulfilling our career aspirations. For us, simply shutting off the birth control switch was no automatic path to parenthood. Conception proved difficult. And when pregnancy finally occurred, there was more disappointment. Two tubal pregnancies and one second trimester miscarriage made it seem as if we were destined to remain childless. Fertility counseling and endless trips to the doctor ensued. Slowly our lovemaking devolved into a means to an end. There were daily temperature readings charted with precision on high school graph paper. This homework assignment was aimed at predicting when ovulation was most likely to occur each month, so we could drop everything and hop into bed. "I don't care if dinner will get cold," I would tell Steve, "we need to do this now!"

There was hormone therapy that made me feel constantly bloated, not exactly sexually attractive. There were fertility tests to make sure my female plumbing was not obstructed and more mildly humiliating tests to make sure Steve's sperm were swimming appropriately. Then there was talk of invitro fertilization or adoption. In fact, it took six years of concerted effort but finally, miraculously, I got pregnant and this one took. In March of 1986 we welcomed our sweet Annie into our lives, miracle of miracles.

Steve took on the role of Daddy with gusto. He could change a diaper like a pro or coax a willful seven-month-old into finishing her mashed carrots without spitting too many spoonsful back at him. Steve often took baby Annie to work with him for a couple of hours while I finished my early morning news stint; the flexibility he enjoyed in his job as alderman was a godsend to this young working couple. And Steve enjoyed showing off his beautiful baby girl to anyone who happened by his office, city officials, business leaders, even local news reporters.

Three months before Annie's first birthday my routine trip to the dentist resulted in an unexpected and truly incredible development. Before taking the dental X-rays, the hygienist asked the mandatory question, "Is there any chance you could be pregnant?"

My immediate response was "No way."

With all the difficulty we had having our first child, birth control was ancient history. Still, I was a few days late in my monthly cycle, so as an extra precaution to my way of thinking, I postponed the X-rays and made a doctor's appointment, just in case. Eight months later, we welcomed Kathleen Gael, all 9 pounds, 14 ounces of her!

Apparently we had somehow solved the mysteries of conception. Molly came along a couple of years later followed by a surprising fourth. Little Miss Colleen made it four children in six years and it was time for another doctor visit, this time for Steve. We had achieved our goal of a big family and neither of us was interested in trying for the boy that so many of our friends were sure we must want. Steve's response to them was always, "I love my girls. Why would I want anything else?"

Besides his young family, another love of Steve's life was running, and not long after we married, Steve somehow convinced me to take up the sport. We clocked many miles together and ran in countless road races. Steve, at a much faster pace, would finish well ahead of me but always circle back to encourage me across the finish line. And as kids came into the picture, they became part of the protocol. We bought a special stroller and took turns introducing little Annie Bananie, and later the younger girls, to the world of running that we both now loved. Steve took to marathon races, though, at 26.2 miles and requiring serious daily training, this was one aspect of the sport I vowed I would never share except from the sidelines with me and the girls cheering him on.

Despite, or perhaps because of our busy blossoming careers, we seized upon any opportunity, any spare moment, to share new experiences with the girls. Bike riding, once a solo escape in search of solitude and a heady bit of exercise pre-children, evolved into a new summertime ritual for Steve. His bike rides now involved pulling a child carrier behind his Trek 12-speed, with his four daughters taking turns, as there was only room for two at a time. I'm not sure who loved these adventures more, Steve or the girls, who often came rolling home fast asleep in the back, an empty bag of candy raisins between them.

Our pre-kids social life of after-work parties, clubbing, and dining out with friends took on a decidedly different air once we became a family of three, and then four, and then five, and six. While not exactly homebodies by nature, parenting, not to mention the steep cost of childcare times four, forced some significant changes in our lives. Movie nights with popcorn in front of the TV after a long week of work and school became a cherished staple. I learned to cook or at least put together a decent facsimile of dinner most nights. Steve often managed homework activities. It was a reasonable compromise to handling two tasks that neither one of us particularly relished.

Our adult social life also became a lot more home-centric. Most often our reward for making it through another hectic work week would be hosting a lively game of poker once the kids were tucked in bed. Steve's mom, sister, brother, and many a friend or two enjoyed, or maybe endured, quarter ante card games that would often go deep into the night, depending on your skill at reading another successful bluff, usually at the hands of Steve or my brother-in-law.

It wasn't perfect, but on the whole we led a pretty charmed life. The family was healthy. The kids had made nice friends and were all doing well in school. My career in TV news was being rewarded with occasional slots at the anchor desk and coveted assignments, including presidential elections and sideline reporting from the field of the 1982 World Series. Not a bad gig for a huge baseball fan. And Steve was settling well into and even enjoying his new job helping redevelopment efforts for the city of Milwaukee, having completed three high-profile, politically successful, albeit challenging terms as a Milwaukee alderman. No one could have predicted the sucker punch that was to alter the world as we knew it.

The happy start of our seventeen-years together. Ever the jokester, Steve loved to point out how his right hand was supporting the cake's top tier which was threatening to topple over.

CHAPTER THREE

THE FUNERAL

"Grief is the price we pay for love."

Gail Honeyman, author

The church was absolutely packed, a standing-room-only crowd. Yet, I barely recognized even a single face before me as I walked up the marble steps to the podium, to the microphone where I would publicly say my final goodbye to the man I'd shared my life with for seventeen years. What an irony to be delivering a message so intensely personal, so intimate, before a sea of others.

I was brief, purposely focusing on Steve's greatest accomplishment, his pride and joy, our four beautiful daughters.

"They are the greatest gift that he ever gave to me and will be a lasting tribute to him," I professed. "I love you, Steve Cullen, and we always will."

No one expected the young widow to deliver a eulogy. Yet it was something I felt compelled to do, having been denied a more private moment to express my love to my life's partner as he died. It was an almost out-of-body experience, one of many that I encountered upon learning of Steve's sudden death five days earlier.

Shock mercifully took over then, as I hung up the phone after the hotel manager finally confirmed the worst-possible news. A numbness settled in, my own sort of pall to settle my nerves and allow me just to breathe. Someone, I can't recall who, managed to tuck my four girls back into bed that night and gradually the house cleared of all the bodies that had appeared on my doorstep within moments of hearing that Steve had died.

"You should get some sleep," Steve's mom Bea admonished me, "you'll need it tomorrow."

Her words, more than those of any other that night, echoed sadly in my soul. Bea had lost her own husband, Steve's dad, to a heart attack at the age of forty-one. My Steve was forty. She knew exactly what lay ahead.

Sleep though, was impossible. A flurry of answerless questions descended upon me. How long had Steve lain in that Cincinnati hotel room before he was found? Was he in pain? Did he know something was wrong but didn't have the strength to reach for the phone to cry for help? Or was death, I hoped, sudden, as the appearance of sleep suggested?

Amid the flood of questions and memories that washed over me in those late night hours, was the nagging replay of a conversation earlier that night with the priest from my kids' school. I don't know who called him or how he heard about Steve's unexpected death, but there he was in my driveway, ostensibly to provide some comfort, some assurances that my Catholic faith would sustain me. Yet the only words I heard were cold and clinical, incomprehensible really.

"We can't have a funeral Mass for Steve at Christ King," Fr. Dennis explained. "He wasn't Catholic, so we can't have his body in the church. We could hold a memorial service, though," he offered weakly.

In that moment, thankfully enveloped in shock, I didn't have the strength or the energy to muster any sort of indignation, to demand that he leave my home immediately. I would never have held Steve's funeral at that church anyway, as I was also a long-time member of a second church, St. Catherine's, and to me that was the only option. My heart was at St. Catherine's, as Steve's funeral would also be.

The fact that this insensitive priest had, within hours of my husband being found dead, rushed over to deliver his indelicate message to the new widow was astounding. Steve's body was welcome in that church when he was alive, sending his children to its school, contributing many dollars in weekly donations and tuition payments. Fully participating in his children's First Communions. Proudly witnessing his young daughters, Annie and Kathleen, sing to the rafters during the annual Christmas programs all bedecked in holiday dresses, and ribbons, and party shoes. Yet, now that he was dead, like a bolt out of the blue, he was no longer welcome. Incredible.

All this and so much more...disbelief, fear, uncertainty, and an overpowering sadness...weighed over me in those hours after family and friends had gone home to deal with their own grief that night. I remember sitting on the couch in my living room looking out the bay window into the street-lit night...looking for what? For answers that wouldn't come? For comfort that seemed so futile? For some reassurance that perhaps I would awaken from this peculiar nightmare wrapped in Steve's arms, all of this a mistake?

It must have been three or four in the morning and my tormented soul was momentarily pulled back into reality to claim a tiny morsel of comfort. A sense of movement outside dragged me from my sleepless trance and caught my eye. There, walking down the middle of the street were two deer. Mind you, we lived in the city of Milwaukee...an urban area boasting a population near 600,000. Deer were not an everyday sighting. Perhaps it was my desperation to find some sense of hope in this impossible situation into which I'd been unwillingly flung. Perhaps it was the anesthetic state of shock that had taken over every neuron in my body. Perhaps it was any number of more logical possibilities, but I chose to see those two beautiful, graceful, wild animals as a greeting from Steve and my mom, who had died seven years earlier. A message of comfort from the two people I loved most in my life, now gone. To this day, every time I see a deer in the city, let alone two traveling side-by-side past my house in the wee hours of the morning, I choose to believe that it's a sort of spiritual hug.

This turned out to be just the first of a number of curious coincidences that took place the next few days as the necessary but dreaded journey of laying my husband to rest took shape.

Early the next day funeral planning began in earnest at my house. One sad, funny, tear-stained task was sorting through boxes of family photos and years of old picture albums, trying to encapsulate a lifetime of Steve's larger-than-life living into six blank poster boards. I have to admit my heart wasn't in it. Luckily, Steve's siblings, his mom, and a few of my sisters took the reins as my ability to concentrate on anything was absent.

This was just one of many sordid tasks to be handled and decisions that had to be made. Not many people in their early forties have a funeral home entry in their contact list, including me, but luckily, my always resourceful sister Joan came through. She reached out to a family friend who happened to be a funeral director. With one call he sprang into action arranging endless details for getting Steve's body back from Cincinnati, writing the obituary for the local paper, working out all the logistics for the visitation and the funeral itself, even handling phone calls from the media who wanted information about the arrangements for this local celebrity. Steve had made the news many times as a long-term political leader, so his unexpected death brought an onslaught of attention. But despite the welcome, take-charge attitude of the funeral director softened by his kind and gentle manner, some tasks still couldn't be completed without input from me. I can remember being led downstairs into the basement of the funeral home to pick out Steve's casket and wanting to scream "I don't care what you put him in. I don't want to be here. This isn't something I should have to be doing."

So many people rose up to help, which is good because I was emotionally checked out. Somehow meals were made and served, the dishes cleaned up. Steve's funeral suit was selected, and his closet, dresser, and medicine chest cleaned out at my insistence. I was so fearful of any memory that might jump out from them falsely giving me hope that Steve really would return at any moment. My kids were cared for, fed, dressed, and bathed. Joan took them out to the nearby private college campus to distract them from the emotions and fears that were eating away at them, too. At ages nine to three, they just needed to run in the sunshine for a short time, to momentarily forget that their lives had changed inexplicably and forevermore.

The next day was typical of early October, warm and bright. Sun-dappled sky peaked beneath the golds, and reds, and oranges of that fall day. At one point in the afternoon, I decided to go for a run, my gift from Steve that turned out to be a godsend that day and so many more to follow.

21

Running quite literally on zero sleep, I needed to clear my head and try to come to grips with this funeral ritual that lie ahead. I can remember only one thing that resulted from that jog. Not how long I'd been gone or how many miles I may have clocked, and certainly not even the route I'd taken, my feet just dictating the course with no direction from mind or body. The one thing I recall with absolute clarity is the formation of a eulogy that I planned to deliver at Steve's funeral. This was nothing that anyone expected or even imagined I might do, but as I ran each step through the neighborhood we'd chosen so carefully together years before to raise our family in, there was no other possibility. There was unfinished business. There were things I needed and wanted to say about Steve and to Steve, things that I couldn't bear to hold silently in my heart. Perhaps Steve's outspoken nature had inadvertently, in the course of seventeen years of marriage, rubbed off on me somehow.

As for the funeral itself, I had already spoken to Fr. Jim, the pastor at St. Catherine's, who was very reassuring.

"We will do whatever you want, Gael. Whatever you and the girls need for Steve's funeral, it's yours."

No questions were asked beyond the simple logistics of what day and time we'd like the service and if there were any particular musical selections we might find comforting. Certainly there was no hint of this Mass for my non-Catholic husband, being anything short of everything St. Catherine's could offer. There was a reason this particular church was my spiritual home.

That same day additional dreaded funeral details again demanded my attention, limited as it was. Arrangements had been made to fly Steve's body back to Milwaukee, but there was a legal requirement that someone...a family member or close friend...actually identify the body. Fortunately, courageously, Steve's brother Tim offered to handle this. In fact, he insisted on it. No argument from me.

I did, however, need to meet with the funeral director to make the final arrangements for the visitation prior to the funeral and the burial after. In the throes of all the shock and disbelief and not-wanting-to-do-this-ever, John Clark was kind, and patient, and so utterly thoughtful. Every detail that didn't absolutely need my attention was taken care of, sight unseen, at least by me.

Because of Steve's stature in the Milwaukee community as a long-time political leader, the pre-funeral visitation was extended to two evenings, to allow for an especially large group of friends, family, and colleagues who were expected to attend. The line was long, stretching out into the parking lot, I'm told, though I was oblivious. As I greeted each person and accepted their condolences or some fond memory of Steve, several people suggested that I take a break or sit down for a while, but I wouldn't hear of it. If my body was physically exhausted, it wasn't registering. I needed to accept every hug, every tear, every small kindness that was offered. Perhaps it was a way of coming to terms with the reality that Steve truly was gone, never to return.

The funeral itself, as with most of the details of those days immediately following Steve's death, was a blur. The church was packed. I know that. Yet if I was asked who was or wasn't there that day, I could only offer a guess in most cases. In fact, the eulogies that were so thoughtfully drafted and delivered by Steve's brother David, by his dear childhood friend Eddy, by my own eight-year-old Kathleen with big sister Annie by her side for moral support, are messages that I now recall only because the church happened to make an audio recording of the service.

Despite the haze of shock that enveloped me that day, I do recall standing before the crowded church, delivering my final good-bye to Steve, with three-year-old Colleen in my arms. "Most of you would know that Steve loved a great party," I began. "He had the habit of being notoriously late to those parties, but he made up for it by inevitably being the last one to leave. Well, he picked a heck of a time to reform himself. This party just won't be half as much fun without him."

The graveside service that followed was an almost out-of-body experience, me watching it unfold but not truly being in the moment for what was transpiring. However, two more curious coincidences did make me smile briefly and reminded me of the invaluable role my faith played and would continue to play in this new chapter of my life. The first was what I like to believe was my mother, Muzzie or Muz, showing up to offer some comfort that day, despite having died herself years before. Her sister, my Aunt Joan, had flown in from Michigan and rushed to the cemetery, her flight arriving too late to get her to the funeral at the church. She pulled up in her rental car and my brother-in-law Bob was the first to notice. The license plate on her car began with the letters M-U-Z.

Then, at the end of the burial service, I had asked that all the kids in attendance, including my daughters, be given a helium balloon. At a designated moment they all released them into the autumn sky as a beautiful, colorful good-bye to Steve. A couple of hours later, back at my house which was a couple of miles away from the cemetery, my nine-year-old Annie broke into a conversation I was having with someone, "Mom, you've got to come outside right now!"

"What's so urgent?" I seem to recall saying, mildly annoyed at the interruption.

"Just come outside. You have to see something," Annie insisted.

Hand in hand, with a trail of curious family following, Annie and I went to the front yard where, locked in the arms of our huge maple tree, were two helium balloons, one green and one yellow. Could they have been from anything other than our balloon release at the cemetery? It was possible. But on a random Tuesday afternoon in October when most people were at school or at work, it seemed unlikely. I chose to believe that was another sign that someone was watching over us that day, a hint that Steve would always somehow remain in our lives, even if he physically wasn't present.

Steve and me in 1993 with the four loves of our life.

Chapter Four

MUTENESS

Muteness. A state of refusing to speak, being unable to speak, or silence.

Vocabulary.com

Death is a difficult subject. No one likes to talk about it. It makes us uncomfortable. But when I found myself dealing with this muteness in various forms after Steve died, it was both confounding and sometimes cruel. One particularly hurtful way this surfaced was in the sudden disappearance of people from my life whom Steve and I had both considered to be close friends.

Before Steve died, a typical Saturday night at the end of a long week, meant letting our hair down a bit. More often than not, the best way we found to do this, to unwind from the stress of meetings and emails, and from carting our kids to their many sports and after-school activities, was a good game of cards.

"Why don't you run to the store and grab some snacks," I would suggest. "I'll put the kids to bed so hopefully they're asleep by the time everyone gets here."

Everyone typically included our usual suspects, Steve's mom, brother, sister-in-law, and a few key friends with enough stamina and quarters to last into the wee hours of the morning over multiple rounds of Texas Hold 'em and 7-card Stud. That often included Barb.

Barb worked alongside Steve at City Hall. Over time, she became much more than just a colleague, joining the close circle of friends that we socialized with, and not just at the poker table. Before Steve and I had kids, Barb became something of a partner-in-crime to me. It was not unusual for the two of us to conspire to get Steve and other friends to check out the newest dance bar downtown, which was something of a feat since Steve hated to dance. But when the DJ started spinning "Stayin' Alive" or "Another One Bites the Dust," there was no keeping Barb in her seat. This slightly crazy, blond bombshell could dance like exploding fireworks, and it didn't take too many glasses of chardonnay for me to attempt to keep up.

Barb truly seemed to enjoy the great evenings we all spent together often over a nice bottle of wine or by exploring a new local restaurant. I thought of her as our mutual friend. Not just Steve's, but mine. That changed instantaneously when Steve died. After his funeral I never heard from Barb again. Not one word.

I understand how words can feel inadequate, pointless. As a news reporter who built a career on the written and spoken word, there was no combination of phrases, no twists of grammar, no clever analogies to even begin to convey the sweeping magnitude of my loss. My heart, my soul, literally felt like one of those explosive bullets had just ripped into my core, shattering into a million fragments, so disjointed, so painful. No amount of talk could convey how I felt or the loneliness and abandonment that gripped me with fear for myself, for my girls, for our future.

Standing at the visitation the nights before Steve's funeral service, it occurred to me that this muteness had struck others, too, in different ways. The line of well-meaning mourners stretched for hours in a long, slow-moving queue. At the head of the line was me, the chief recipient of condolences. Some would express their sympathy and admit, as I could so well appreciate, that words were failing them. Others let a long, teary hug say what they could not. Still others managed to resurrect a funny Steve story or a fond memory to help ease the awkwardness of that painful moment.

But it was the muteness after the funeral, the muteness of friends like Barb and others, that made me profoundly sad. I understand that death, particularly a shocking, unexpected, painful one invoked on someone so young, can leave many of us confounded by what possible words can be said to bear any sense of comfort. We all struggle with our own personal grief.

But what was so perplexing to me was that some ignored the topic altogether. There were people in our social circle with whom Steve and I had shared many a wonderful, spirited evening, often over a great meal at a new local restaurant. People who had labored generously, tirelessly to help Steve's political campaigns. People we considered close friends. When they completely turned away after Steve's death, perhaps consumed by their own grief or foolishly hoping that I might have it in my reserves to somehow comfort them, it compounded my own loss. Somehow it seemed I didn't have value in that friendship now that Steve was no longer a physical part of it. Perhaps just the sight of me or my girls was too much of a trigger, a reminder of the friend they had also lost. So their response was to just walk away.

Others danced around any conversation that might involve Steve. "Don't say anything, or it might set Gael off and she'll cry," was a common refrain.

While that could be seen as a magnanimous gesture, I resented it. A, it's ok to cry, even healthy to cry, and B, let me decide what I want to hear, even if it causes me some sadness. Honestly, the best gift anyone gave me for years after Steve died was a great memory or a funny moment that spoke to his peculiar, sarcastic, witty personality or some kind deed remembered and shared.

My response was at once protectionist and perhaps even a bit selfish. I was not going to have Steve lost to my girls or me any more than the sudden cardiac arrythmia had already done or the unrelenting passage of time was bound to do going forward. I was determined to keep Steve's memory alive. When Steve and I were in the first blush of dating, I'd ask him about his family, his father in particular, who had died when Steve was only seven. At the time, it seemed a little odd that Steve could only tell me a few basic facts about his dad, where he worked, where he grew up, but not much at all about his personality or what he loved most about his father or the times they shared. I learned years later that Steve and his siblings were specifically told, by whom I don't know, not to mention their dad after a heart attack claimed him at age forty-one.

Steve's older brother Tim told me he and his five siblings were cautioned. "We were told that if we even said our dad's name, it would be too hard for our mother to bear."

No wonder little seven-year-old Steve carried so few memories of his dad to share with the woman who would become his wife, and ultimately his widow, too.

I was determined that my girls would not endure that same fate. I made a point of talking about Steve with them and encouraging them to do the same. We regularly pulled out old family movies to catch a glimpse of Steve or delight in the warmth of the laughter that he would so often share.

Each year on Steve's birthday we would hold a special celebration in his honor and everyone would share their favorite "Dad" story, a tradition we carry on to this day. In the company of friends or family I would never avoid mentioning Steve, and, in fact, I often went out of my way to bring him up, to give license to others to do the same... to quell their muteness in a way. My throwing Steve's name into a conversation might have been awkward for others at first, but as a result, my girls, now adult women, have a treasure trove of shared memories to draw on when the need or the moment calls for it.

Others picked up on this private quest for Steve memories and offered their own stories on any number of occasions. One particularly treasured collection of these came in the form of an unexpected present two months after Steve died. Unbeknownst to me, Steve's younger brother, David, had mailed letters out to dozens of family acquaintances, old friends and relatives, near and far, asking them to share any Steve memories they'd like. David then compiled all of these written accounts, photos, and even physical mementos in a beautiful scrapbook that he gifted me and my girls with for Christmas. The book was filled with delightful stories, many from people I didn't even know, people who had been impressed by Steve's kindness or touched by his wicked sense of humor at different times over the years.

Many were stories I had never heard before. One favorite was from an older gentleman who knew Steve as a neighborhood kid who went to school with his son, and, years later as his alderman. Karl was seventy-five when he passed along a Steve story known only to him.

"I'm in my thirty-first year of running, having long passed my prime," Karl wrote. "So when Steve overtook me along Menomonee River Parkway, as he often did, he could easily have cruised on by. But he always adjusted his pace down to mine and we would continue to run in tandem while discussing marathon running and other equally vital subjects of the day!"

There were other stories of Steve's generosity, many of which I knew, but reading them from the recipients of his kindness added an extra sparkle to the memory. There was the time Steve managed to score Neil Diamond tickets, including backstage passes, to Milwaukee's annual summer music festival. His "dates" for the evening were Big Julie, a colorful friend of his mom and former bar lounge singer, and my sister Pat, who flew in from Michigan for the occasion to see her forever hero on stage. "Cracklin' Rosie" and "Sweet Caroline" never played to two more adoring fans, and creating the chance to meet Mr. Diamond in person was almost as big a joy to Steve as it was to Big Julie and Pat.

Music and rock concerts were a passion of Steve's, and they were often the subject of his largesse. Not long after the Neil Diamond gift, Steve arranged another equally magnanimous present, taking my oldest sister, Joan, to her first ever concert, to see Paul McCartney. As big as this show was for any old school rock 'n roll fan, this particular act of kindness came at a significant time. Joan's twenty-year-old son, Collin, had just been diagnosed with cancer, and all the scary details of his treatment and sleepless nights of worry weighed on Joan immensely. Steve's gift of a night with "the cute Beatle" was a welcome diversion.

Steve always delighted in making people smile and showing them a good time. His sense of humor was recounted numerous times in our book of memories. One friend's story made me laugh out loud, not an easy accomplishment with Steve's loss still so raw just two months out from the funeral. The friend, who helped preside over our wedding, remembered asking Steve quite seriously why we had chosen October to get married, expecting some sober, thoughtful response.

"And without missing a beat," the friend wrote, "Steve replied that October was a good hair month for him."

A former colleague who served on the common council for many years with Steve gave my girls a great sense of their Dad's legacy.

Tom Donegan wrote, "his mouth was quick, his mind was quicker and his heart was kind."

"Steve's many qualities," Tom continued, "included his sense of joy, his love of family, and his courage to do the hard things for the City of Milwaukee because they were the right thing to do."

Perhaps the most poignant Steve memory came from Molly's kindergarten teacher, and it was one that, until reading it in the scrapbook, was totally unknown to me. Ms. Schutz told of five-year-old Molly's excitement during a class trip to the pumpkin farm the day before Steve died. "I can't wait to show my daddy my pumpkin," the teacher remembered Molly saying. "You know he comes home tomorrow." Molly never got to show her dad the pumpkin lovingly cradled in her arms.

Colleen's high school graduation with good friends
Carol and Eddy. Eddy was Steve's buddy in high school
and remains a steadfast and loyal support to our family,
always ready to share a quick "Steve story."

CHAPTER FIVE

LONELINESS

"The loneliest moment in someone's life is when they are watching their whole world fall apart, and all they can do is stare blankly."

F. Scott Fitzgerald, author

November, 1981. Steve and I were traveling to Michigan to spend Thanksgiving and my birthday with my family, two great justifications to load up the car and drive 400 miles, at least as far as I was concerned. Steve was happy to placate my desire for family time at the holidays, but to be honest, what clinched this road trip for him, was Mick Jagger.

"I scored two tickets to the 'Tattoo You' concert on December first," Steve proudly announced one evening shortly after Halloween. "And it's in Detroit, at the Pontiac Silverdome, so we could make a long weekend of it."

Smart guy, that Steve. He knew I wasn't too keen on long drives in November's very changeable Midwest weather, but combine the Rolling Stones with mom, dad, and sister time, and I was an easy sell. Plus we loved sharing rock concerts together and the Stones were one of those bands that had been on our bucket list for ages.

By a stroke of absolute luck, our general admission tickets landed us in seats that were maybe two dozen rows from the stage and up high enough that we could see and hear every move, every strain, every strobe light effect to "Start Me Up" and "You Can't Always Get What You Want."

"I could throw a basketball from here and hit Mick Jagger," Steve exclaimed over the chants of the exuberant crowd.

I was completely caught up in the moment and in the heart-pumping excitement of sharing it with my young, would-be rocker husband. We never sat down, dancing to every beat, our voices growing hoarse from cheering, our hands red from clapping. When the concert ended as it had to on "Satisfaction," Steve and I were equally drained and energized. Experiencing that Stones' concert alone would have been great. Experiencing it with a guy who absolutely grabbed life by the horns and lived it to the max brought an energy and excitement and, at times quite honestly, a level of exhaustion, into our life together.

Loneliness seems such an obvious, painful result of losing someone you love so deeply without ever having the chance to say goodbye. Yet the complexities of that loneliness, even with the passage of time, were hard to wrap my head around. For someone who likes to plan, to control the course of events, this loneliness thing was an untamable tiger. There was no predicting it, no steeling oneself for when it might attack. Certainly it was always lurking, simmering beneath the surface much of the time, especially at first. But it was the sudden onslaught of emotions and memories that were the toughest to tame. At times they could paralyze me or prompt angry outbursts or moments of inconsolable sadness in my girls.

For me, this overpowering sense of loss was often triggered by something seemingly innocuous, especially at first. A song on the radio could evoke a sudden crying jag. "The Boss," Bruce Springsteen, a fixture in our musical tastes as a couple and subject of dozens of shared, hard-rocking, dancing-on-the-seats concert memories, was notorious for this. Just the first note or two of one of Springsteen's anthems on the radio would force me to have to stop whatever I was doing in that moment to collect myself.

Other times it was a visual cue. I remember driving down the road running errands one day, and suddenly seeing a billboard of one of our favorite restaurants pop up before me. I was instantly so distraught, gulping for breath through uncontrollable sobbing, that I had to pull over for fear I'd cause a traffic accident.

A busy day at work or the kids' crazy, hectic schedules of soccer, and scouts, and school helped keep the loneliness at bay much of the time, but it never went away, particularly in those first days, weeks, and months after Steve died. Every time a car would pull into our driveway, one of the girls would leap up, sure it was the sound of their favorite car, Steve's funky old gray Cadillac, driven by their favorite guy, only to be disappointed again and again. That disappointment grew into absolute desolation at times. The girls, all nine and younger, didn't understand this concept of loss and their gut-wrenching sadness was compounded by a very real sense that no one understood what they were going through, no one at school, none of their friends, not even me in many ways. My loss was different. I hadn't lost my Daddy.

A couple weeks after Steve's funeral, three-year-old Colleen asked me, as she had ever since she was able to talk, if I would "send Daddy up when he gets home." On first blush, it crushed me to remind her that I couldn't do that, much as I wanted to. But it was also oddly comforting, in a way. I wanted so much for those parts of our routine not to be lost. I wanted the girls to know their dad and remember the tremendous love he had for them. I didn't want them to forget counting down the days, as I did, until he'd return from an out-of-town business trip. Or the playful horsing around, the way he would hold each one of them when they were little and toss them high in the air as they squealed with delight (and I cringed). Or "Friday movie nights," complete with popcorn and admission tickets crafted by one of the older girls.

Now facing other parts of our old routine absent Steve evoked a strong sense of trepidation. I never knew if or how I might muscle through these moments alone. Three weeks after Steve's funeral, the usual suspects, family mostly, were back at the poker table on a Saturday night at my house. The usual suspects minus one, of course. This night was bound to happen sooner or later, as spontaneous weekend card games were such a regular affair at our house. So I braced myself for the evening, relying on the thought that in some way it might be good to be surrounded by family and close friends carrying on in Steve's memory. The game turned out to be okay. Not too traumatic. Honestly quite the opposite of the night before.

I had picked up the girls from school and daycare and gotten dinner on the table, probably a lasagna or a taco dish from some kind person still on the meal train that so often follows a death. I don't remember anything specific that touched it off, but all of a sudden, totally out of left field, I was drowning in a wave of loneliness so powerful and yet so paradoxical. On the one hand, I had my four beautiful daughters clamoring for my attention, yet all I wanted was to be left alone. No one, not them, not anyone, could fill the desolate canyon of grief created by Steve's loss. I found myself wanting to run away from this godawful situation, from the kids I loved so much. It didn't make sense.

My desolation in that moment reminded me in a curious way of a heart-wrenching story that had hit the news just a couple months earlier. A young mother in South Carolina had been convicted of buckling her two young sons into their car seats and then pushing the car into a lake, drowning them. Initially she had contemplated driving the car into the water, ending her life as well as her sons', but for whatever reason she didn't do that. While I could never have contemplated hurting my girls or myself, I had to admit feeling some odd sense of empathy for that tragic situation, some appreciation of the concept of all of us, together as a family, suddenly rescued from our own tragic loss in one dramatic moment. The pain ended. The crushing loneliness conquered.

Haunting thoughts were just one manifestation of this beast of loneliness. Other times it revealed itself as a kind of paralysis. Many times I would find myself frozen, seemingly incapable of managing even the smallest task, of pulling together even a simple bit of our daily regimen. Packing lunches for school the next day could seem like climbing Mount Everest. In my head I knew this was silly. It shouldn't be an issue. Yet I would find myself completely stuck with no energy or ability to follow through. I would try to hide my distress from my girls, thinking they wouldn't understand. I didn't want to place any additional burden of my loss onto their own. But my very perceptive daughters weren't easily fooled. I remember one particular incident where Molly, at just five years old, had the insight to know that Mom needed more than her well-intentioned hugs could provide. She convinced her big sister Annie to call Aunt Joanie, and get my sister to come over to help rescue Mom from her "black hole."

Another time, Kathleen had just returned home from a week at Girl Scout camp, perhaps ten months after Steve's death, and she had something special for me. She had made me a bracelet of red beads that she said represented a wish for love.

"You keep it on your wrist until it wears down and the beads fall off," Kathleen instructed me. "And that wish will come true when that happens."

I was amazed at how perceptive she was. I tried so hard not to openly express my loneliness too often in front of the kids, my heart-wrenching ache for Steve. I didn't want to magnify their own loss. Yet, they knew. They felt it. We all felt the sadness of the mounting time without his jokes, his laughter, his sarcastic wit, his love. It didn't need to be verbalized.

Even the youngest, Colleen, was not immune to the loneliness of missing her daddy. One night, out of the blue, my little three-year-old woke up hysterical and disoriented, worried that her sister and roommate, Molly, was not in her bed. Molly was there, of course, just snuggled beneath the covers. Still, it made me appreciate how deep this loss goes. Colleen, like the rest of us, was truly afraid of losing anyone else in her life without a moment's notice.

There were many of these quicksand moments, not just for me, but for all of us trying to cope with Steve's loss. And not all occurred in the immediate aftermath of his death. Nearly two years later, as Kathleen was finishing fourth grade, her teacher came up with a class art project parodying Time Magazine's Man of the Year edition. She thought it would make a nice Father's Day gift for each child to make their own "Father of the Year" booklet. Then she insisted Kathleen had to pick someone else to write about because her dad wasn't alive to receive this gift. Sadly, I didn't find out about this insensitive episode until the project was already complete, coming home in Kathleen's backpack. The protective momma bear came out in me when I saw it. Angry, I wanted to call the teacher on the carpet that very moment and let her know in no uncertain terms that Kathleen did have a dad, alive or not, whom she should still honor with this tribute. But I didn't need to act on my instincts. My resilient eight-year-old had handled the situation on her own, making her beloved Aunt Joanie her "Man of the Year."

Still, the singling out of Kathleen for being different from the others in her class, a difference she hadn't chosen, pained me. I pictured her, ever the adult-pleaser, trying not to cry in front of her classmates. Not to tell her teacher she was wrong, insisting that she should be able to memorialize her dad. While this particular incident was emotionally wrenching, it was not unlike one that played out in many ways for each of my girls. None of my kids knew anyone who had lost a parent, no one their own age who could begin to imagine the depth of their loss. There were a few cousins whose families had changed because of divorce, but to my girls, that form of separation wasn't in the same universe as having your playful, funny, loving father stripped permanently from your life in one terrible instant never to be seen again.

Over the years, I tried many ways to help the girls cope with their loss. Certainly there was therapy. Many different therapists. Many different coping strategies. But one of the best things I ever did for them occurred almost by happenstance. This was before the internet, before Google, and it must have been desperation that drove me to, of all things, the Yellow Pages. Who thinks of a fat, yellow advertising directory as a source for grief groups for children? And yet, amazingly, there was one entry that seemed to hold some promise. A Lutheran church in a nearby suburb offered a gathering one night a month specifically for children who had lost a parent. Fully expecting resistance from my girls, and not sure myself if this was a good idea, I gave them no option. We would give this group a try and after two sessions if they didn't find it helpful, they could call it quits. That ultimatum proved unnecessary. The girls absolutely loved the chat circles, the art projects, the role-playing that they did side by side with other kids whose mom or dad had died. It was the first time they found peers who could relate to their own experience, and they to theirs. Not only did we go back after the mom-mandated initial two sessions, but my kids anticipated these monthly gatherings for the next two years, cultivating tools that helped them cope with their loneliness in the years that followed after they aged out of the grief group.

That same strategy didn't work so well for me, at least at the outset. One of the attractive features of the kids' group was that this same church offered an adult grief group on the same night. This seemed perfect. Not only would I not have to find somewhere and something to occupy myself for two hours waiting for the girls' session to end, but I might find some comfort for myself at the same time. I went exactly twice. The group consisted of a lot of people who had lost a sibling or a parent, not the kind of loss I was experiencing as a forty-one-year-old widow with young children. There were a few in the group who had lost a spouse, but they were all generations older than me. When they would describe how their intense grief made it difficult to even get out of bed in the morning, I could not begin to relate. With four little kids nine and younger, I would have loved an excuse not to get out of bed, but that was not my reality on any level. This new life did not allow me any opportunity to hibernate beneath my covers, perhaps catching just a little more sleep, but more likely escaping, even for a few extra moments, from the onslaught of daily responsibilities and challenges that come with being a single mother.

As fate would have it, I was not the first nor the only one to dismiss the adult grief group as irrelevant. A handful of other newly-widowed young mothers dropping their kids off at the children's group started talking. They had tried the adult group, too, but decided it wasn't for them. What began as awkward, momentary encounters among strangers soon evolved into long conversations at a nearby restaurant, sharing our frustrations, sadness, loneliness, and fears about raising our children single-handed, or dealing with the financial strains of being suddenly reduced to one income. Over cups of coffee or an occasional glass of wine, we shared stories, hugs, and tears, always coming away from these informal monthly gatherings with a sense that we were not alone on this journey. We bonded over our shared losses and drew strength from each other, tapping into reserves of resiliency we didn't know we possessed.

My kids also taught me a lot about resiliency, a gift from some higher power that we, at various times, were able to tap as we laid claim to our grief. Four years after Steve died, Colleen used a school art project to give shape to the loneliness that she hadn't quite been able to describe in words, and her innermost fears of forgetting the Daddy she'd only known for three brief years. All the other second graders used "The Magic Wand" assignment, proudly posted on their classroom walls for the school's open house, to wish for new bicycles or trips to Disney or the latest Atari video game. And then there was my Colleen. Asked to complete the sentence "If I had a magic wand...," she, in her best seven-year-old printing unabashedly wrote "I would use it to make my Dad come back from Heaven."

The Magic Wand
by Colleen Cullen
If I had a magic wand
I would use it to make my
DaD come back from Heaven

Seven-year-old Colleen's most magical wish, entirely
unprompted, made her classmates' desires for new
bicycles or trips to Disney seem trivial.

Chapter Six

UNCERTAINTY

"Life is about not knowing, having to change, taking the moment and making the best of it, without knowing what's going to happen next."

Gilda Radner, comedian

Paper. So innocuous. So utterly non-threatening. Yet as I sat at my kitchen table trying to sort through the piles of documents needing my attention those first days after the funeral, I was paralyzed by uncertainty. It was hard enough just trying to figure out what to wear each morning. Even remembering that I should probably eat something for breakfast took about every ounce of my limited attention span. To tackle the mountain of legal paperwork before me was impossible. Life insurance forms. Employee compensation. Ordering the official death certificate. And then my favorite, writing a few key descriptors for the gravestone. How do you possibly sum up your husband's whole life in a phrase? It all needed to get done but I just couldn't focus. Perhaps in some way dealing with all these details meant accepting that Steve was truly gone. I wasn't ready.

It felt like I'd been thrown overboard in a rough sea, gasping just to catch my breath. Stress and uncertainty had become part of this package of grief that I was forced to unwrap in the completely unexpected loss of my husband and best friend. Steve was so central to life as I knew it, to my past, to my present, and certainly to what I had envisioned for my future.

I was left with a tangle of questions so enormous that it seemed beyond anything I could even begin to handle. Did we buy enough life insurance or save enough rainy-day money to help me navigate a suddenly uncertain future? With the wanton, immediate loss of half of our family's income, would we be able to survive in any way close to the lifestyle we knew? Could I possibly manage to keep us in our family home, the only home any of our girls had ever known, or would the reality of our new financial circumstances force us into something much more modest to make ends meet? Perhaps we might even be faced with the cold slap in the face that we needed a different neighborhood, away from family, friends and neighbors we'd come to love, in order to find housing that was now affordable? And what about my daughters' education? We had been fortunate enough to eke out parochial school tuition each year, agreeing that our girls would be well served in a place that would nurture their spirituality as well as their educational prowess. Would that now have to take a back seat to more immediate needs like heating the home, paying the water bill or putting food on the table?

Then there was high school looming in the not-so-distant future. Annie was just five years away from that milestone. Steve, brought up a good Methodist, had somehow convinced himself that his daughters should attend the highly-rated, all-girl Catholic high school in the area. He had been impressed with the college prep education and the strong leadership skills instilled in two of our nieces at that school and he wanted nothing less for his girls. I, on the other hand, having eight years of uber-strict 1960s Catholic education under my belt, was not so convinced that we should subject our daughters to that scenario. It was a discussion to be had later when Annie reached eighth grade. But now that decision would rest on me and me alone. Would I honor Steve's wishes? Could I even afford to honor them?

Complicating this overwhelming concern about our family's future was the reality that I didn't have a firm, detailed grasp on where Steve and I stood financially when he died. I was the one who handled the day-to-day expenses, making sure the utility bills were paid on time and that the mortgage was covered. Steve couldn't have been bothered with such minutia, but give him a line a hot stock tip that would certainly make us rich, or at least a bit better off, and he was all in. While I enjoyed the benefits of a wise or lucky investment in the stock market, I had never been one to dive deep into the nuances of *The Wall Street Journal*. To me, business news was boring.

So Steve would often come to me, the pragmatist, to see if we could scare up a few extra bucks for some promising investment. If he could present a good case without forcing me to read some dull prospectus, we'd make the move. These were never large investments, perhaps a few hundred dollars here or there, but with a growing family, it was our way of saving for those far-off expenses like college for the kids and eventual retirement. As a result of this balance of financial powers, I had only a passing knowledge of what exactly we owned, investment-wise and where specifically it resided, when suddenly my money manager was gone. Talk about stress.

One thing I did know was that we had purchased some life insurance, though the details of the plan were a bit hazy. Steve and I had spent considerable time debating the need for this and putting up with an over-eager agent intent on making a sale. Steve fell on the side of it being a good investment. I, only in my twenties with no kids at the time, felt a bit more invincible and questioned whether this added expense was truly worth adding to our monthly budget. Fortunately for me, Steve, once again, made a convincing argument and we signed onto a policy, partly, to my mind, to get the obnoxious agent to stop badgering us. Twelve years later when Steve suddenly died, the policy essentially paid off the balance on our mortgage. Losing the house was at least one worry that was taken off my plate.

As for the sudden loss of Steve's income, that was a more pressing concern. Steve was definitely the major breadwinner in our family. At the time he died, I had moved on from reporting and the embarrassingly sub-par wages of TV news. I loved my role as a journalist, but had faced the hard reality that I was not destined for the anchor desk, the only news job that came with fancy contracts and impressive salaries. So I moved on to commercial video production, doing occasional public television documentary work to satisfy my journalistic heart while also producing training videos for a large healthcare entity that happened to be headquartered nearby. It was steady work at reasonable pay and I enjoyed it, particularly because it was part-time, allowing me to be home after school when my kids got home. My nagging fear was that I would now be forced to find a new full-time job giving up that all-important family time in search of a larger paycheck that would support our family of five. That would also entail finding good after-school care that wouldn't break the bank. The anxiety ate away at me. The 'what if' and 'how do I' questions kept me up many nights. I felt lost and totally alone.

Luckily, a trusted friend who worked in finance saw my distress and came to my rescue, throwing me a proverbial lifeline. Jim had me pull together every bit of financial paperwork I could lay my hands on so he could figure out exactly where I stood financially. While I never bothered to read any mail with even a hint of investment jargon in it, at least I knew enough not to throw it out...ever. Many a dust bunny was set free as I purged through my old file cabinet. I compiled for Jim a huge mishmash of tax records, life insurance documents, bank statements, and prospectus reports dating back years from a half dozen different brokerage firms that Steve had used over the course of our marriage.

Presented with this daunting array of paperwork, I was shocked that Jim didn't regret his kind offer to help.

"It's not as bad as it looks," he lied. "Give me a couple of days and then I'll let you know what I've found."

Three days later, after gamely poring over the mountain of records and shredding what was no longer needed, Jim had my financial world organized into one neat, manageable file, one that even my non-business mind could follow. He walked me through it all and recommended ways to consolidate it so I wouldn't face a monthly avalanche of statements anymore. Ultimately, he put one very worried young widow at peace.

"You're actually in a very secure place, financially," Jim advised. "Let me walk you through it and answer any questions you might have."

First off, an education fund had been set up for my girls after Steve died. Countless friends and family had made generous donations and, while it wouldn't begin to cover all their college costs, it was a good head start, and Jim would see to it that the money was invested wisely so that it would grow over time.

Then another unexpected windfall.

"You know you qualify for Social Security, right?" Jim said.

"I'm a long way from sixty-five, Jim. What are you talking about?" I replied.

"No, this isn't your retirement benefit. You and the girls qualify for death benefits based on all the years Steve paid into SSI," Jim explained.

It turned out, after filling out the proper paperwork, a one-time widow's benefit would be mine. Even more amazing was that each of my daughters would get a modest monthly stipend from the government until they were eighteen. I felt the weight of my financial yoke easing off my shoulders.

As for my investment portfolio, it turns out Steve had made some decent purchases in bonds and a few stocks. It wasn't a huge amount of money, but Jim assured me, with a few adjustments here and there, they were the basis for a decent savings toward my ultimate retirement. In the meantime, between Social Security and my working, particularly if I could bump up my hours to full-time, we could manage just fine. No major life changes required. It was as if one dark, threatening storm cloud had begun to lift. My future and that of my girls was not at risk, at least from a financial perspective.

A family trip to Disney World, minus two-year-old Colleen, when life seemed so sure and promising. Steve died ten months later.

Me and the girls on a major road trip out west in 2004, an adventure that included white water rafting down the Colorado, an all-natural rock water slide outside Sedona, our first rodeo, and, of course, the Grand Canyon.

CHAPTER SEVEN

FEAR

"I learned that courage was not about the absence of fear, but the triumph over it."

Nelson Mandela, Former President, South Africa

Fear of being a good mother, or at least an adequate one, was not a product of Steve's sudden death. Even with my partner by my side, there were occasional moments of self-doubt, like the time Steve wanted me to join him on a business trip on the eve of Molly's first birthday.

"I've got a conference for work in Denver in a couple of weeks and I want you to come with me. It's supposed to be a really great city." Steve, always the master of persuasion was trying to convince me that a long weekend away from the kids would be a good thing for us both.

"But we'd be gone for Molly's first birthday," I argued.

"Molly will never know," Steve quickly replied. "And we can celebrate with a big party when we get back."

I had to admit I was intrigued. His flight was already paid for, as was the hotel room, and the conference agenda was fairly light, leaving us ample time to discover a cool new city at the base of the Rocky Mountains. I tamped down my motherly guilt and agreed to make childcare arrangements and get time off work.

Then, within hours of us landing in the Mile High City, my sister, who was babysitting, called. Molly had chicken pox. If there was any doubt, it evaporated instantly. I was a failure as a mother.

Now, in hindsight and in fairness to myself, that was certainly an over-reaction. Molly survived just fine, and in fact, probably would never have known her parents abandoned her sick little self were it not for the telltale red blemishes on her face in her birthday photos that year. Denver moments happen. It's part of the parental job description. You must be prepared to consider your own inadequacies and somehow rise above them.

But rising above was not an option after Steve died. Abject fear set in. Being a mother was hard enough when you had a partner to shoulder the responsibilities and even share in your periodic failings. Being absent that half of the parental unit was terrorizing. I was afraid I would never be able to teach my four girls everything they would possibly need to know as they became young women. I worried that I wouldn't be an adequate role model for what they might hope to accomplish in life or how they might accomplish it. Steve's death heightened my Denver inadequacy barometer exponentially.

My family's financial security was also something that kept me awake at night. Losing Steve's income meant going from 32 to 40-plus hours a week, a major adjustment in terms of my being available to my girls. My boss was willing to be as flexible as possible, but video production, for the most part, was not something you could do remotely, and it rarely ended promptly at 5p.m. I stressed about the potential downsides of my additional time at work.

I could extend the hours for my youngest who was in home daycare with a woman I liked and trusted. That was easy. But the other girls were in two different schools, one of which was more than a mile from home. The logistics of finding decent sitters who could bring them home each day and at least get them started on homework assignments was daunting.

The most obvious choice was to hire seventh or eighth graders from their schools who wanted to earn a little extra money. On its face that sounded doable. In practice it was not so simple. Finding reliable sitters without after-school activities of their own who were willing to watch three very active younger kids five days a week was next to impossible. I ended up cobbling together a bank of different prospects and then juggling the schedule week after week to make sure everyone was on the same page of who had who when. And heaven help me if any of my kids had scouts or another after-school activity to complicate the process. My stress meter bounced off the high end on a regular basis. Eventually, my network of friends and family connected me with a high school girl to be my consistent single baby-sitter, and she could drive. An absolute lifeline.

But even with the best of babysitters this business of working full-time was draining. I would get home after a long day and immediately have to confront one very basic need. It was suppertime. These kids needed to eat and dinner wasn't going to make itself.

Afterwards, homework called. As one who never graduated past stick figures, helping with paper mâché volcanos and Native American dioramas was challenging on a good day, and next to impossible when my brain was spent after a full day at work. Even tasks that should have been easy sometimes managed to become difficult.

"Mom, you don't borrow in subtraction," my third grader informed me, rolling her eyes. "It's called regrouping."

Apparently, simple arithmetic had evolved beyond my capacity, college math major notwithstanding.

From homework there were baths to administer before tucking all four children into bed. Then it was on to catching up on laundry and packing lunches for the next day, which was a trick of its own. I had to make sure to remember who would only eat grape jelly with her peanut butter sandwich and who wouldn't touch the sandwich if even a hint of any jelly made it onto the bread. And don't *ever* make the mistake of putting cherries in Molly's lunch or a banana in Colleen's.

All of this made for an exhausting routine. By 9p.m. most days, my time and energy were spent. I had to get to bed so that I could handle a repeat performance the next day.

My fears were not just about having the stamina to maintain this busy, bordering-on-insane schedule. I worried that I might not have enough reserves to do a decent job of parenting, to craft a good life for my kids in the absence of their dad. If all my kids saw in me was a tired, stressed out, sometimes crabby mother, that seemed a huge injustice. How was I to guide them and steer them toward positive, fulfilling futures if my own example was that of a harried, half-crazy person always trying to do too much?

Then there was my own pressure to step into Steve's shoes, to attempt to fill the gaping hole left in my girls' young lives. There were many aspects of Steve's presence, of his personality, that I felt I was inadequate to convey. One perfect example, was his sarcastic wit and his ability to find humor even in the most challenging circumstances. Not long after his death, Molly, whose given name is Mary, turned six. I had tried to make the weekend extra special, knowing how desperately she was missing her Daddy on her big day, but it wasn't working. Molly was out of sorts and crabby all weekend. On Sunday, her actual birthday, there was a brief hailstorm, so I seized the moment to try to make her smile with my best Steve-ism.

"This crazy June weather is a message to you from Dad," I told her.

Then, mustering up an old Catholic prayer that she knew from school I told her "It's his way of saying 'Hail, Mary!' on your birthday!" I'm not sure Molly appreciated the humor.

Beyond no longer being exposed to their dad's unique sense of humor, there were far more significant worries that I had for my now-fatherless kids. My daughters had been cheated in life, stripped of the one man who shared their DNA and had their best interests at heart, who loved them to his core. I felt it was somehow my duty to fix that. So I purposefully set out to try to bring father figures into their lives, a foolish exercise, it turned out. An uncle, godfather or family friend would occasionally step in to take one of them to a Girl Scout dance at school or invite them to a sporting event, but while the girls might have had a good time in the moment, I soon realized it was impossible to manufacture a connection that just didn't exist. All of my daughters knew that the guys taking them to these events, as well-intentioned as they were, were only placeholders. There was no substitute for their dad.

Another fear that gnawed at me was that my girls wouldn't have firsthand exposure to a healthy marriage to model in their own lives as they grew older. I wasn't sure how I, now only half of a couple, could teach them what they should expect, or most importantly, what they deserved in a relationship with any guys they might date. I was so far from being ready to re-enter the dating world myself, that I felt ill-equipped to help them handle the complications of male/female relationships, let alone to be any sort of model that they might emulate.

To varying degrees I saw each of my daughters impacted by this void in their lives as they became young women. Molly later admitted to me that she struggled with relating to the opposite sex, unsure of herself in the company of any guy beyond the shallowness of sexual attraction.

"I wasn't seeking the right relationships and I think that part of that is because I didn't know or have a healthy male relationship in my life," Molly told me. "I still feel like I'm kind of uncomfortable around men because I didn't have that growing up."

It was a helplessness that would hit me time and time again as each daughter ventured into the dating world. I couldn't show them by example what goes into a loving, positive relationship with a man, and no amount of mother/daughter talk seemed up to the task of offering them this important guidance. As my teenage girls would have expressed with dismay, words of advice from mom were just lame. Tackling my financial fears paled in comparison to these less tangible ones, ones that would affect my daughters far into the future. I would find myself continually questioning my ability to handle this parenting responsibility alone.

Colleen, Annie, Kathleen and Molly celebrating Annie and Kathleen's college graduations from two different universities on the same day, making their single parent one proud momma.

Chapter Eight

DEPRESSION

"We did not feel prepared to be the heirs of such a terrifying hour. But within it we found the power to author a new chapter, to offer hope and laughter to ourselves."

Amanda Gorman, American poet

Milwaukee's Lakefront marathon had become a regular entry in Steve's annual running calendar. He never made a big deal about it, but I knew, and the kids knew, this 26.2 mile commitment every first Sunday in October was something he wouldn't miss. And it became something of a family affair. For days before this important feat, the girls would gather around the kitchen table while Daddy was at work, up to their elbows in poster boards, colorful markers, glitter glue, and a myriad of stickers. We had secretly conspired to surprise Steve on race day, showing up at significant mile markers along the route to cheer him on.

After Steve left early on Sunday morning, I bundled the kids up, grabbed all their colorful signs, and headed to the 5-mile mark, timing it so we'd be firmly planted on the roadside when he passed by.

"Way to go, Dad."

"You can do this."

"We love you, Daddy.'

Once he passed by, we'd quickly jump back in the car and head to the 10-mile mark, or the 20-mile mark, or, eventually the finish line. The kids were so excited to see their dad on his annual mission. And he delighted at seeing them along the route, always managing a huge grin despite the increasingly achy, tired muscles that were the price you paid as a marathon runner. Steve's last marathon was four days before he died.

In losing Steve so unexpectedly without the chance to say goodbye, I found myself subconsciously looking for any facts or hints or impressions that might somehow give me the closure that I ached for. The funeral home offered me the option of identifying the body once Steve was flown back from Cincinnati, but I couldn't bear the thought of seeing my once vibrant husband in whatever god-awful state he might be in two-plus days after dying. Even the funeral home director had warned me that Steve's body might be bloated, and discolored, and that rigor mortis would surely have set in. The idea of that being my final image of Steve quite honestly turned my stomach. I had so many wonderful ways to remember him, so many times of joy, and laughter, and love. I feared seeing him in the cold, harsh basement of a funeral home would somehow erase those other images. My need for closure wasn't worth that risk.

Still there were so many "what if" questions that ate away at me and my girls. What if the hotel made a mistake? What if Steve really was delayed by business in Cincinnati? What if he had just missed his flight? I mean, this was a guy who had run a marathon just four days earlier. How was it possible he could be dead?

In those few months following the funeral the impossibility of Steve's death would creep back into our daily lives. Every time a car pulled in the driveway, my heart would skip a beat, thinking, just in that instant, that Steve was finally home, only to be momentarily disappointed by the sister or friend who then walked in the door. Every now and then I'd see a figure in the distance who bore a slight resemblance to Steve in the cut of his hair, or the way he strode, or his build, and I'd move closer for a better look and the inevitable disappointment.

When, seven weeks after Steve's death, a thick manila envelope appeared in my mailbox bearing the return address of the Cincinnati coroner's office, I opened it both with trepidation and anticipation. I was sure that the autopsy report would finally give me relief, an explanation of why my forty-year-old husband had been snatched from our lives. That was not to be. Instead, even to my untrained eye, the pages written in formal medical-ese seemed to indicate that Steve's body was "normal" in most every way. The worst thing the medical examiner found was one artery that was 50% blocked. "Heck," I thought. "One of your brother Tim's arteries is 80-90% blocked and he's still here to talk about it. How is that fair?"

I wanted answers. Perhaps my amateur reading of the autopsy findings was missing something. There had to be a reason for an otherwise healthy young man to just collapse and die. I turned to an acquaintance who happened to be a doctor.

"Would you read this, please, and tell me what you think," I asked. It didn't take long for his response.

"If I didn't know better," the doctor told me, "I'd think this was a report on someone who's still walking around. There's no indication here of why his heart just stopped."

Dissatisfied with that response, I set out on a mission of sorts to try to explain Steve's death. It was a mission destined for mediocrity. Of the many doctors and medical experts I consulted, the educated consensus, which felt like more of a guess to me, was that his death was probably caused by sudden cardiac arrythmia. Like an electrical switch that just flips, instantly shutting down. A blown fuse shutting off energy to the body in one single, final, nearly always fatal act. It was not something that could be stated with certainty, the doctors told me, as it is impossible to diagnose after death. And considering the fact that only one percent of people stricken with such an arrythmia survive and then only if they happen to be in a hospital at the time it hits, this information brought precious little comfort and no real sense of closure.

Perhaps my quest for closure was a mistake. It probably intensified my grief and sent me burrowing deeper and deeper down the rabbit hole of despair. There were days and so many nights when the bleak emptiness, the fear, the overwhelming sense of loss consumed me.

"I hate that you're not here," I wrote in my journal. "Everywhere I look I see you, but I can't hold you or hug you. I hate this life."

Certainly the suddenness of Steve's death was part of it. The all-consuming despondency that it triggered nearly sucked the lifeblood out of me. It was much more than a matter of bad timing. We had, for seventeen years, built a life together, created a legacy together. Our four young daughters were thriving and bringing us joys that we never anticipated. We had supported each other in crafting our respective careers, Steve as a rising star in local politics and me as a reporter and occasional anchor at a well-respected local TV news station. As young newlyweds and with each successive day and year that our marriage achieved, we fully expected that someday, far down the road, we would walk hand in hand into our twilight years, still occasionally jabbing each other with inside jokes and the self-deprecating humor that we loved about each other.

To have that vision coldly and cruelly unplugged, even eviscerated, launched me into a state of panic. A state of interminable uncertainty. A state of depression.

I experienced many of the telltale signs. When I returned to work, I had tremendous difficulty concentrating on even the simplest tasks. Trying to tackle a lengthy, complicated script for a video production was futile. It was so counter to everything I knew, to everything I was. All of this fueled my feelings of being lost and helpless.

Outside of work, I was always tired and often irritable. I lost interest in the basic mechanics of living. Something as simple as enjoying a home-cooked meal brought no pleasure whatsoever. And the idea of putting up a Christmas tree or decorating for the holidays that followed soon after Steve's death left me feeling only empty, vacant.

Many times I questioned my worth as a now single parent. How could I possibly be capable of raising four impressionable daughters alone? All the responsibilities of that mission were daunting enough when I had my partner by my side. Did I possibly have it within me to deal with my girls' every need, to be their primary teacher and role model in life, to help shape their futures? The self-doubt ate at me.

I don't think I was ever suicidal. I would never abandon my daughters. Yet there were occasional fleeting thoughts of wondering if everything might be better if the girls and I could just go down in a plane crash together. Or if we could somehow jointly experience what had happened to Steve, a flipped switch that would instantly, painlessly shut off our hearts so we could be done with all the wretchedness of this new reality we were living. And there were many nights I cried myself to sleep, if I was able to sleep at all. Fortunately, my own deep sense of responsibility to my daughters always gnawed at my subconscious and helped me maintain a reasonably good front at least for them. Still, I wasn't fooling anyone. Not myself, and certainly not the sisters and closest friends who recognized that I needed help to pull me back from the edge.

In a logical world, the idea of seeking professional help to recover from a major trauma was wise and probably necessary in many cases. But logic was not at all at play here. I felt a little like I was looking at life through a kaleidoscope. Everything was distorted. Nothing made sense anymore. It was all I could do most days to handle the basics of getting the kids off to school in reasonably clean clothes and making sure there was food in the house. Whatever focus I could muster, to my mind, had to be on my kids and their needs. They were my first priority, my only priority after Steve died. It almost didn't occur to me that I might benefit from talking to a skilled counselor. Plus, honestly, finding a therapist that my insurance would cover who might connect with me and my particular situation was off-putting. It was one more demand on me between full-time work, all of my family obligations, and the need for child care if I was ever to have even an hour or two devoted just to me. There were plenty of excuses not to seek that outside help.

It was my sister, Joan, who helped me see the light. She led the charge in getting me to realize that the magnitude of coping with this grief was not something I could do alone, that it was anything but selfish to make myself a priority.

"You're not going to be any help to the girls if you're not well," Joan would admonish. "You need to take care of yourself."

It was a phrase that was echoed by other family and friends time and again and again and again. I think it may have been less about heeding their sound advice and more about getting them all off my back that finally pushed me to look into counseling.

It's not like Googling "plumber" when you have a leaky faucet. Finding a therapist is complicated. With such deeply personal issues and heartache in play, it didn't seem right or productive to just throw a dart at a list of family counselor names and see what stuck. One friend was a great resource. As an attorney who regularly helped clients navigate their ways not just through the court system, but also through personal issues, she had encountered her fair share of counselors. And she understood my loss completely, as she was also was dealing with the countless issues that confront a suddenly single mother. Her own husband had recently died, too. Her advice was able to at least get me started, steering me toward therapy practices with good reputations and competent practitioners.

The first psychologist I saw seemed promising. She was knowledgeable, not effusively warm or uncomfortable, and she was able to dive into the deep end with me fairly quickly, uncovering a multitude of insecurities and anxieties that had found fertile ground in my post-Steve psyche. I can't say I looked forward to our sessions together. I was still pretty raw around the edges and talking about it was hard work. Still, she gave me some tools, some coping mechanisms that seemed to help. It was when we inevitably ventured into my relationships with my kids that I began to question some of the advice I was being given. One particular moment stands out.

Annie, our oldest, had been dealing with anxiety attacks and I wanted to understand how I might help her. The therapist suggested Annie join me in a session, which she did. The conversation quickly turned to the therapist asking my young daughter what she thought would make her life easier, what would help calm her nerves. When a perplexed Annie came out with "I don't know," the therapist unhelpfully wondered if a pet might help. This came totally out of left field for me and my immediate thought was "Sure, just what I need, another living being to take care of right now." Before I could raise my own concerns with this suggestion, the therapist was offering my now-very-interested nine-year-old a couple of gerbils that she happened to have and was looking to give to a new home.

Bert and Ernie soon came to live with us against my better judgement. Inevitably, as it does with most kids offered a pet, the vows of "I'll take care of them; I promise," soon dissolved into me nagging Annie about cleaning the gerbils' cage or making sure she didn't forget to feed them. If there was any therapeutic value to this pet ownership experiment, it was soon lost. Bert and Ernie, it turns out, were in reality Bert and Ernestine, and before we knew it there were nine baby gerbils added to the mix. What a sweet way to teach a pre-adolescent about the facts of life, one might argue, to help her get over her anxiety. Not. It seems gerbils have the repulsive habit of eating their young. Try explaining that to a nine-year-old. There were only six babies left one day. Four the next. Soon they were all gone. At that point even Annie agreed that the remaining parent gerbils had to go. We found them a new home.

For me, my work with a new therapist ended almost before it began. I was overwhelmed with the litany of responsibilities that was my life. Raising four kids alone, kids who all had difficulty dealing with the loss of their father. Making sure these kids got a good education. Being their go-to resource for any homework challenges or special projects. Getting them to and from all after-school activities and a growing list of recreational sports that involved juggling four different practice and game schedules, depending on the season and the sport. Laundry times five. Grocery shopping and preparing meals. The list was endless. And throw full-time work into the mix and it seemed insurmountable.

Knowing that there wasn't any way to take most of this off my plate, therapist #2 suggested if I could find some stress reliever perhaps it would at least become more tolerable. The suggestion itself was well intentioned but I was skeptical.

"That all sounds good," I suggested. "But my go-to stress reliever is running. How do you suggest I do that when I'm with four kids, ages three to nine, every waking hour of every day?"

"What about hiring a babysitter?" he suggested.

"Finding a sitter at a moment's notice when my stress level is going through the roof is not an easy thing," I explained. "I need relief daily, even hourly some days. Even if I had a sitter at my fingertips, I couldn't afford that."

"Well, Annie is almost ten, right?," he offered. "What if you just did laps in front of the house or loops around the block? I agree it's not as good as a long run, but couldn't she keep an eye on the other kids knowing that you were just outside?"

"You're forgetting one critical thing," I responded. "Annie won't let me out of her sight because of anxiety attacks. She absolutely would freak out if I left the house."

The therapist agreed that was problematic. Then he offered a solution that almost made me laugh out loud. I was supposed to set my alarm for the middle of the night, get up and put on my exercise clothes as if I were going jogging. When Annie woke up, as she inevitably would being a light sleeper, I should tell her I'm going out for a quick run, but then not actually go, sending her back to bed. After enough nights of this routine, he assured me, Annie would begin to dismiss any fears about my running. I had a hard time following this logic or accepting that this approach would do anything more than make an already overwrought, stressed-out mother even worse off for lack of sleep. I left his office and never looked back.

Eventually I found another therapist who was wise, and kind, and truly helped me gain perspective on the challenges I was facing. Between her professional help and the amateur counsel of close friends and family, the dark days of depression lifted and I found myself better equipped to handle the new curveballs that life inevitably sends our way.

Steve's last marathon in 1995. A passion for running was a gift that he inspired in me.

Chapter Nine

ANXIETY

"So when my mom would drop me off at school I wasn't able to leave her side because I was so worried something was going to happen to her."

Annie Cullen, age 9

Annie was in first grade. Being our eldest and starting at a new school that fall, we were still getting used to the plans for hot dog lunch, which day was library day, and the need to pack a second pair of tennis shoes specifically for gym day, pristine enough so as to not scratch the floors as her class learned the intricacies of dodgeball.

In addition, there were these things called demerit sheets, a completely novel concept for us fresh out of the simpler, innocent days of kindergarten. Every week these sheets would come home in your child's backpack noting any incidents of poor behavior or missed homework. By signing the demerit sheets, you as the parent were attesting to the fact that you had reviewed the transgressions and taken any appropriate action.

Annie seemed to be settling in well at her new school, so I was surprised when Mrs. Mike called one day.

"Did you happen to see Annie's demerit sheet this week," her teacher asked. "It was supposed to have been returned today?"

"Oh, I'm so sorry," I apologized. "We're still getting used to everything with a new school and all. I'll ask her for it when she gets home today."

Which is exactly what I did, only to be informed that "I left it in my desk, Mom. I'll bring it tomorrow."

Tomorrow came and went and this demerit business quickly fell off my radar. Then another call from school.

"Hello, Mrs. Cullen. I'm sorry to bother you again, but it's about that demerit sheet of Annie's," Mrs. Mike started.

But before I could muster up an excuse probably worthy of its own demerit, Mrs. Mike cut me off.

"I just wanted to know if you usually sign your name in orange crayon?"

It was all I could do to keep from laughing out loud. My little six-year-old who was still learning to print, much less write in cursive, had cleverly figured a way around this demerit business. Steve's reaction was similar when I told him about the orange crayon. As parents, we knew we had to muster up some righteous disappointment over her handling of the situation, but secretly we were both impressed. This was a kid who would be able to take the world by storm someday. Until her world collapsed around her.

One huge concern for myself and my kids was anxiety. I had no psychology training beyond a couple of classes in college, but I began to think of fear as a kind of pyramid. The foundation of this pyramid was worry, something that nags at you, but kind of rides in the background of your mind, annoying but not too disruptive. Ratchet that up a level and you found stress, worries that had pushed more front-of-mind and might even be starting to impact you physically. For me personally, stress tended to gnaw at my stomach and I would not eat much, or, on the flip side, I'd take comfort in junk food rather than the healthy meals I knew I should be eating. At the top of this unfortunate pyramid was anxiety, where the fear of some perceived danger could intensify so greatly in the moment that outright panic would set in. This pyramid of fear moved in with us after Steve died, affecting each of us in different ways at different times, but none may have been as troubled as my Annie.

At nine years old, Annie was a bright, fun-loving kid who loved shooting hoops in the backyard with her Dad, going on bike rides, and playing soccer, preferably as a forward, always aiming for the goal. Our backyard jungle gym was a favorite haunt, shared, almost always amicably, with Kathleen, just seventeen months her junior. Annie was a good big sister and seemed to especially relish the responsibility of caring for any of her three younger sisters as Mom's helper. She also had a circle of very close friends and loved the camaraderie of Girl Scouts, if not all the work of earning those darned activity badges. Annie's self-confidence did her well in school where she was respected by classmates and teachers alike. She loved spending time with cousins, both in Wisconsin and in Michigan, a common destination for family trips. Growing up as the eldest in a loving family, hers seemed an easy, carefree life.

Whether it was her place as number one child or their shared love of sports, Annie was definitely Daddy's girl. They had formed a bond that made me a touch jealous at times. I wasn't sure if it was her seeming preference for Steve or his for her that made me more envious. Then, in an instant, it all blew apart. The impact on my Annie was heart-wrenching and startling.

With Steve's death, my strong, take-on-the-world fourth grader was suddenly transformed into a puddle of nerves and anxiety. When she returned to school for the first time after her dad's funeral, Annie clung to me as I tried to leave her in the parking lot. Where normally she would have immediately run off to connect with her friends with barely a "goodbye, Mom" to me, she absolutely refused to get out of the car. I finally dragged her into the building, still Velcroed to my side, weeping, and trembling, and absolutely distraught. Once outside the classroom door, I had to call her teacher into the hallway with one of Annie's most empathetic friends. Eventually, together, we were able to coax Annie inside. I was beside myself, exhausted, and completely perplexed by this stranger that had taken over my daughter's body.

And this wasn't just the first day back at school. When this same scenario played out every day for one week and then two, I was beyond worried. I was totally lost as to what was going on with my daughter or how I could help her, and she couldn't seem to express to me why she was so terrorized. I reached out to my wise older sister Joan, so often my sounding board. I thought as a teacher, she might have some insights.

"You really need to get Annie some professional help," Joan advised. "I know there are therapists who specialize in treating kids who've experienced trauma. Let me chat with my teacher buddies and the school counselor and see what they recommend."

It turned out Annie was having anxiety so intense that it triggered these schoolyard panic attacks. Through therapy she was ultimately able to explain what was causing this paralyzing distress and to learn techniques for coping with it. It was not, as my unprofessional diagnosis might have thought, that the panic was a result of her missing her dad, her favorite guy on the planet. No, it turned out she was afraid of losing me and was unable or unwilling to share that with me.

What triggers an anxiety attack is intensely personal and may seem unreasonable to an untrained observer. I remember assuring Annie that I was just going to work when I would leave her at school, and that I would be back afterwards to pick her up, as I had done ever since she started school. But no amount of logic worked. Annie was dealing with a level of distress so great and so real that it paralyzed her, interfering with her well-known routines, her closest friendships.

"You just feel like whatever moment you're in, you need to get out of the situation or the place or whatever it may be," Annie would later tell me.

And there were physical symptoms, too, not just emotional or psychological.

"You get like this tightness in your chest and the shoulder pain," she explained. "You can get dizzy, and lightheaded, and feel like you're going to pass out for no reason."

Unfortunately, Annie's panic attacks were not limited to those first weeks back at school. Where she had never had an issue before, new fears emerged. Flying now terrorized her, even though she'd ridden on planes without any problem since she was a baby, accompanying me back to Detroit to visit my mom, and dad, and sisters many times. And then there were elevators. I had to assure Annie that we would stay on the lower floors of any hotels when we traveled because the mere thought of getting into that enclosed, moving metal cubicle was more than she could handle. Her panic was overwhelming.

"Just those few seconds feel like forever," Annie would tell me. "I would not wish this on my worst enemy."

As she got older, well into her teenage years, the anxiety still haunted her. She was constantly worried about being left alone. Annie couldn't babysit for her siblings, even if I needed to make a quick run to the grocery store, unless she could call a girlfriend to stay with her. Sleepovers, the hallmark of adolescence for most girls, were a no-go. Even in high school, where annual overnight retreats were part of the curriculum and peer pressure to participate was enormous, Annie's anxiety would gain the upper hand. She'd set out to the retreat center accompanied by her closest buddies, but invariably I would get a call in the middle of the night from my weeping, panicked daughter and I would have to drive out and collect her.

"It was the fear of doing things that kept me from doing everything," Annie would tell me.

All of this brought more therapy with different therapists over the years, some of it helpful, others not so much. Sometimes it was individual counseling for Annie. Sometimes it might be family sessions that included me or her sisters or both. When she'd find herself in a particularly anxious time, we even went the route of medication, but that didn't seem to help. As one of those parents who always wants to "fix" things for her kids, I felt I was failing my daughter. I was desperate for any solution that might resolve this turmoil sprung from the aftermath of death, any way to return Annie to the carefree, stress-free world she had known before she lost her dad.

Over time, Annie's mental anguish improved dramatically, not from any magical "cure," but in her learning to recognize when a panic attack was coming on, and in her own resolve to keep it at bay, to not let it control her life. These attacks still rear up occasionally even in her adult life, not as frequently and, thanks to her coping mechanisms, not as severely, but they have become an unwelcome consequence of her grief journey.

Even as a parent herself, Annie will find herself projecting her fears onto her own children in situations they might be experiencing.

"When I think about my son going on sleepovers, that makes me anxious," Annie says. "But he's fine. I pray every night that my kids don't ever have to deal with this anxiety bullshit that I have. I hope they get their dad's laid-back personality."

In a curious way, life sometimes helps you turn lemons into lemonade as the old adage goes, and that has been the case with Annie. Working as an athletic trainer at her old all-girl high school, she sees lots of students who are experiencing high levels of stress and anxiety. She's found that sometimes sharing her personal battles with fear helps her athletes as much as taping up a sore muscle or diagnosing a possible concussion.

"When they come to me in the middle of a panic attack, I can tell them that they're fine, and we can walk through it, and get them calmed down," Annie will say.

She appreciates her athletes' concerns about appearing weak to their teammates who don't understand what panic attacks are or how debilitating they can be.

"So I think that makes me very relatable," Annie explains. "Having had so many panic attacks myself, I can help them realize that nothing bad is actually going to happen to them. Like, they're not going to pass out. They're not going to die. So just take a deep breath."

Going for a bike ride with her favorite guy. Steve would often take Annie and her sisters out for a spin on a summer afternoon.

CHAPTER TEN

ANGER

"Anger is a symptom, a way of cloaking and
expressing feelings too awful to experience
directly – hurt, bitterness, grief and, most of
all, fear."

Joan Rivers, comedian

It was a cold, typical Wisconsin winter night in December,
two months since Steve died. I'd worked all day. Picked up
the kids from school and the sitter. Thrown some kind of
dinner together, probably broccoli-stuffed chicken breasts
from Market Day, a godsend of prepared foods offered
through my church that were moderately healthful and
quick to cook. And it was snowing. Again. Forever the snow.

Exhausted by the day, the dinner hour and the rituals of
getting four kids tucked into bed, appropriate stories read,
and nighttime prayers said, I wanted nothing more than to
sit down and put my feet up, perhaps even indulge in a tiny
cat nap before starting preparations for the next day, another
school day. That meant signing any homework or notes that
each kid may have had from their teachers, making lunches,

familiarizing myself with any schedule amendments that would require some other arrangements for sports or Girl Scouts or after-school snacks.

And then, the snow. There was nothing unusual about this particular winter storm. When you live in Milwaukee, that comes with the territory, several storms over the course of the seemingly endless winter that stretched from late November often well into April before releasing its icy, cold white grip from your bones. You get used to it. But that particular night, as I trudged outdoors at nearly 10pm to clear the sidewalk and the ever-so-long driveway by hand for the umpteenth time, I was angry.

"You should be here doing this," I shouted into the winter sky, not caring if any neighbor was witnessing this slightly crazed woman in her snow-filled driveway. "This is your job, not mine!"

Tears streamed down my cheeks with each shovelful of the heavy, cold annoyance. Steve had always taken care of the outdoor chores that came with owning a house. I handled so much of what needed to happen inside, that it seemed a good working compromise. How dare he leave and dump this wet, sloppy, heavy burden on me?

Of course, it wasn't really about the snow. It was yet another slap in the face, as if I needed it, reminding me that the house, the kids, the financial worries, everything sat squarely in my lap. Steve was not there to shoulder any of the mountain of responsibilities. The one who for seventeen years had been by my side, was noticeably, prominently, permanently, awfully absent. He hadn't asked for this, but neither had I. It seemed ridiculous to blame Steve for putting me in this mess, but I was mad and didn't know how to tame the anger boiling over inside of me. I had to direct it somewhere. So the unrelenting onslaught of snowflakes became my target.

There were many points in time when anger rose up and threatened to throttle any one of us. My kids were just as vulnerable as me and, like me, ill-equipped to know what to do with this raging monster that would hover just below the surface waiting for a moment, an occasion, a time least-expected to rear up and lash out. Each of the girls responded differently to this anger, both in the immediate weeks after Steve died and at various times in the years that followed.

Annie would fold into herself. Never one to confront other people or her emotions, she would often go quiet and insist nothing was wrong, in defiance of the inward anguish you could almost palpate. On the rare occasions that she would express what was in her heart, she might ask "how do you really know Daddy died? How do you know that wasn't just someone else they sent back to us from Cincinnati?" She was angry. Angry at God for taking her daddy from her. Not understanding how a supposedly loving God could do that to our family. I wished I had better answers for her questions. Ironically, the one whom I normally would have consulted to decide how best to handle these "tough issues" was himself the source of them. I hated not being able to talk to Steve about Annie's anxiety.

Kathleen, on the other hand, released her anger and fears by completely launching herself into random acts of kindness. It was her way of defusing an untenable situation. The night of Steve's funeral after an outburst over some small thing, she told me that her "pressure was just too high." And, largely on her own, she found a coping mechanism. She became that kid, and later that young woman, who was the first to volunteer if anyone needed help, even if they didn't know they needed it. She was the thoughtful one who, even as a young teen, would remember birthdays or write spontaneous notes of encouragement to a circle of friends that grew wider and wider and wider and included growing ranks of adults whom she impressed with her boundless largesse.

Little Colleen, only three when her dad died, admitted to being "mad at Daddy" when I would tell her for the umpteenth time that he wasn't coming home. She kept insisting that Daddy must be in jail, a place where he just couldn't come back, much as he would want to. I guess she figured if Heaven was such a good thing, certainly whoever was in charge would allow Steve to come home where he belonged. She wanted desperately for her dad to be "un-dead," figuring with each new day that it must finally be time for "Daddy to come down from Heaven."

And then there was Molly, my little rebel. Steve had nick-named her Taz, as in Tasmanian Devil, when her stubborn willfulness would drive him crazy. Ironically, she was the most like Steve in terms of personality. From her first words, Molly always said exactly what she was thinking, no holds barred, and there was no convincing her that her opinion might be in any way flawed.

"I don't like bewwies," eighteen-month-old Molly might say, swiping the strawberries and blueberries off her highchair tray onto the floor.

There was no convincing her otherwise.

"You don't negotiate with a terrorist," was Steve's only half-joking response. He and his precious Molly understood each other.

Coping with the death of her beloved Daddy was more than my five-year-old could begin to comprehend. How could she? She didn't know how to confront this enormous loss, how to speak to the heartbreak inside of her. So as usual, Molly's response was anger. She tended to lash out, often about things that seemed trivial, masking the true source of her outrage, the unfairness of losing her dad.

These angry outbursts started just weeks after the funeral, when the glaze of shock started to peel back revealing the ugly, raw nerves that came with reality settling in. It was no momentary upset. We all had that. But for Molly, her anger often rose to the level of outrage, lashing out verbally, physically, emotionally. There was yelling, screaming, and hateful words unfurled, though usually retracted later. And it was something that would seem to crop up out of nowhere. Taz on the loose.

Three months after Steve died, not long after I had returned to work, we had the opportunity to spend a winter weekend at a lodge near Lake Geneva, a beautiful little resort town in southern Wisconsin. It was a get-away completely paid for by my company as a holiday gift to the staff and we were encouraged to bring our kids to enjoy sledding, skating, and cozy snuggles by an outdoor fire pit, not to mention the indoor heated pool.

But what was meant to be an idyllic retreat turned into a nightmare. I'm sure we were all feeling out of sorts taking our first family vacation without Steve, but no one made it more clear than Molly. She was having no part of it. Molly's anger boiled over into outright tantrums several times and I lost control, yelling and crying, and ultimately locking us all in our hotel room, afraid to let any of my co-workers see the ugly mess that was our life in that moment. I couldn't wait for the weekend to be over. Had we not hitched a ride there with another family, I would have checked out that first night and slunk back to the privacy of our home, demoralized by my inability to calm down my raging five-year-old or tame the anger and helplessness that her fury brought out in me.

As Molly grew older, the hateful, destructive eruptions seemed to take a turn toward rebellion, against me, against school, against most any rule that anyone tried to impose upon her. Some of this might have been normal teenage angst, but it rose to such a level that I felt there had to be more at play. While I didn't like to use Steve's death as an excuse for bad behavior by any of my girls, there was little doubt that figured into the equation in a big way for Molly. She carried with her an enormous fear of losing any memories of her Daddy, a fear compounded by each passing year. She would get indignant if anyone suggested she might not remember him, knowing in her heart of hearts that they were right. What does anyone remember of being five years old? It took a long time and several rounds of therapists for her to come to grips with that.

Years later, at nineteen, Molly found a small way to make sure everyone knew that her dad was still permanently in her heart. She secretly sought out a tattoo parlor and had "ár m'athair," "our father" in Gaelic, inked onto the nape of her neck, knowing I was not a fan of tattoos. While I initially wrote it off as another sign of rebellion by my daughter, I later came to appreciate it as an important statement for her to make on many levels. It was one way for her to honor her dad and his memory as her life moved forward without him.

Molly's rebelliousness made high school a huge disappointment, at least for me. Here was a kid who normally collected top grades like Halloween candy. She rarely had to study and aced every exam, no matter the subject. She was particularly keen on the sciences and talked earnestly of one day becoming a doctor. Yet with each new semester, particularly as she got into her junior and senior years, the grades tumbled. Cs and Ds became the norm and no amount of cajoling, praising, bribing or grounding made any difference. Molly began hanging out with a group of kids I didn't know from the grocery store where she worked after school. I suspected there was drinking involved, hoped there were no drugs, and more than once discovered she had snuck out of the house late at night to go who-knows-where with some new "friend." Molly would later own this rebellion.

"I feel like I grew up very sheltered," she told me. "And the more limitations that you put on someone, the more they want to break out."

Molly's high school years were followed by a tumultuous college experience. I insisted that all of my girls live on campus during college, even if they stayed in Milwaukee. The idea was for them to develop personal and financial independence. To learn how to make good choices. To understand that they had to live with the consequences of their actions, whatever they might be. It was a part of their education, I figured, equally as important as whatever they would learn in the classroom.

For Molly, that real-life education was met with a lot of resistance, complicated by OCD. While Molly was never officially diagnosed with obsessive-compulsive disorder, even she admitted that her way of coping with stress was to shop, and to shop to a level that didn't even make sense. Her purchases were way over the top, both in volume and in frequency. She just couldn't control herself.

Freshman year the credit card companies discovered this vulnerable new eighteen-year-old, and she was a willing target. My repeated warnings that the credit card wasn't a free pass to acquiring any new bauble that struck her fancy fell on deaf ears. At one point her spending got so out of control that she burned through the money I'd given her to pay her tuition. That was the last straw. I cut off her college funds. If she was to stay in school, she'd have to figure out how to manage that on her own.

Money problems were not the only issue for Molly. A fraternity party resulted in a harrowing and demeaning attack. She got no support from the university but, sadly, was afraid to reach out to me until long after the incident. Her grades suffered, and she dropped out of school with a huge pile of debt and a demoralized sense of self-worth. No amount of praise or heart-to-heart talks could help me convince my bright, talented daughter that she was not a failure, that her future still held so much promise. I felt that I had failed her as a parent. It wasn't the first time I would question my own ability to shepherd my daughters successfully and safely into adulthood, and it wouldn't be the last.

With all the mother-daughter battles Molly and I struggled through during her high school and early college years, gifting her with her beloved Reggie was one major victory...for us both.

CHAPTER ELEVEN

ACCEPTING HELP

"I struggle with weakness, shortcomings and inadequacies, and yet I resist asking for help. Please teach me to humble myself and cultivate the practice of seeking help from others."

Maria Shriver, author

I was on a return trip from Florida where my good friend Kathy and I had taken our six little girls for Easter vacation. Kathy was also a widow with young children whose husband had died just months before Steve. Since we were first introduced two years earlier, we had rescued each other from countless moments of worry and anxiety, often through tears, as well as laughter. We had learned to accept help from one another without judgement or question. So strong was our bond, in fact, that Kathy had no problem almost literally pushing me off the packed airplane when we paused in Chicago for a layover. The airline was offering free tickets to the first five volunteers who would give up their seats, right then and there.

"Get off the plane now," she insisted. "If you take Maria and your three older girls, we'll have five tickets for next year!"

The next thing I knew, I was on a Greyhound bus from O'Hare to Milwaukee with four little girls in tow, fueled by Cinnabons that somehow seemed an entirely appropriate use of our airport food vouchers as we dashed off. The fact that I didn't hesitate to complete the final leg of our journey home from Florida in the dark of night via the bumpy toll road of Interstate-94 spoke volumes about the value of friendship.

One of the hardest things for me to do after Steve died, was to accept the love, and support, and help that was offered me, well beyond the flood of wonderful ready-to-eat dinners that church and school friends dropped off in the weeks immediately following the funeral. I had always been a pretty fiercely independent person, so it may have been silly pride or my dogged determination to handle everything on my own, but I had a hard time learning to not only accept help that was offered, but to even seek it out. It took a while, but I soon realized I needed to come to terms with the fact that I was not Wonder Woman, especially in the face of such a monumental loss for the girls and me, and that this was not some failure on my part but a very important way of owning my grief.

For each of the friends who stepped or slipped away after Steve's death, there were countless others whose kindness, wisdom, and amazing generosity of spirit and time helped hold our family together as we forged this new life together. Some were family members, as you might expect, who always seemed to know when a phone call or an unplanned drop-in visit was needed. My five sisters were uncanny in their ability to do this even though all but one lived hundreds of miles away. They could hear something in my voice on the phone or sense a particularly stressful time with the girls, and they were always there to offer guidance and relief, not to mention an occasional kick in the pants.

"You've got to take time for yourself, Gael," they would say. "You'll be no good to the girls if you're stressed out and can't cope."

Often this advice would be accompanied by a gift certificate for a massage or an offer of free babysitting so I could get a run in to clear my mind or even just make a trip to the grocery store without children pulling at me, demanding some treat or the latest brand of cereal.

Steve's family, too, while dealing with their own deep loss, managed to help me and the girls deal with ours. I wasn't sure how or if my in-laws would respond now that Steve, our common bond, was no longer there. Yet they did. Sometimes this took the form of play dates for my kids with their cousins to give me a break from the non-stop duties of solo parenting. Sometimes it was vanquishing my house of a sudden, smelly infestation of chipmunks that had made their way into my heating vents. (Sorry, Chip and Dale!) And then there was a newly established ritual of Tuesday night dinners at my brother-in-law and his wife's every week – one night when I could actually end a long day of work with a hot, home-cooked meal for me and my kids that I didn't have to shop for, or prepare, or clean up after. They continued this lovely gift for years, along with the gift of their steadfast company, until their kids and my own became so busy with after-school extra-curricular activities that it no longer made sense.

Beyond family, loyal friends stepped up, too, but in ways that were often surprising and so very generous. One, in particular was Steve's childhood friend, Eddy. With no kids of his own, Eddy somehow found it in himself to quasi-adopt mine. Wednesday night's basketball league was one great example of this. Organized years before by Eddy with several buddies including Steve, Wednesdays had always involved a night out with Daddy, at least for my older girls. Steve would take the girls out to dinner (perhaps a bit of a stretch when it usually meant McDonalds or Cousins' subs) and then bring them to basketball, where they and the other fathers' kids would play until the hoops competition was done for the night. After Steve died, Eddy picked up the ball, so to speak, insisting on continuing this Wednesday night tradition if the girls and I didn't mind. To this day, Eddy and his wife Carol remember every one of my girls on their birthdays and other significant occasions, subtly making a phone call or dropping off a card to let them know they're in their thoughts. This generosity of spirit is remarkable. I deeply appreciate it and my girls are touched by this continuing connection they have to their dad through this kind and thoughtful longtime friend.

There were many surprising pillars of support that helped us through some dark and challenging times, too; new people who entered our lives and quickly became part of a solid support system for both me and my girls. There was Denise, the mother of a transfer student, Betty, whom Colleen befriended in fourth grade. When Denise learned of our family's loss years earlier, she insisted that she was going to pick up and drive, not just Colleen, but all four of my kids to school every day, to take that task off my shoulders. There was no discussion. Denise, and later her daughter, continued this chauffeuring all the way until Colleen and Betty graduated high school.

Many others also randomly appeared in our lives, making our life-without-Steve a bit more bearable. There was the soccer coach or random parent who would call to insist they were driving one of my daughters to a game or practice without me having to ask. With all four of my girls playing soccer on different teams with different game and practice schedules, these calls were a godsend. Then there was a newly-discovered relative-in-law who connected with me after moving back to Milwaukee from out of state. She would constantly "check in" inviting me out to a girl's lunch that she would never allow me to buy. Or the neighbor whose backyard pool always welcomed my daughters and often their friends, any time the weather permitted.

This process of owning grief by recognizing and accepting new sources of support opened me up to Kathy's friendship, something that was totally unexpected, and, as it turned out, a lifeline. Shortly after Steve's funeral, I received a call from my sister's friend John, the funeral director. He insisted that there was someone I really needed to meet, another young mother with a sadly similar story. She had two little girls and had lost her husband to a heart attack just a few months before Steve died.

"The two of you have so much in common," John said. "You really should connect."

In that moment, I was skeptical. I had enough to deal with I thought, going back to work full-time to support my family, navigating all the school and after-school activities of my kids, just living this new life that my heart wasn't accepting. Why did I need one more distraction in my life, one more person who might want some piece of me?

I had amassed an amazing, caring, insightful support system in my family and close friends. Yet, I had to admit there were instances when I didn't believe that they could truly appreciate the insecurities, the anger, the anxiety, and the magnitude of my loss, hard as they might try. In many ways I felt that I was flying solo, with no one to appreciate the struggle that I faced as I awoke each morning. So the idea of meeting someone who was truly walking in my shoes piqued my interest. I took down this woman's phone

93

number. It was perhaps one of the best things I ever did to lay claim to this grief and not let it claim me.

Kathy was the woman on the other end of the phone call I made the next day. Her seemingly healthy husband had died of a sudden heart attack in May, five months before Steve's heart called it quits totally out of the blue. Kathy's two young daughters fit very neatly between my girls in age. Maria, was just younger than my eight-year-old Kathleen, and Emily, just younger than Molly and ahead of my three-year-old Colleen. Kathy worked full-time as an attorney and was attempting to juggle the demands of work under this new mantle of single motherhood. And it was a struggle. Clearly we needed to talk. We arranged to meet for coffee the next day.

When I arrived at the coffee shop still holding onto a pinch of uncertainty for what I was about to get myself into, I was surprised to find myself greeted by not one, but two young mothers. Kathy quickly explained that John, the funeral home director, had also introduced her to Cheryl, whose husband died of cancer shortly before Kathy's Tom had passed. Cheryl had three sons, just slightly older than Kathy's and my kids. While I found this young widow-matching service a bit curious, I tried to remain open-minded.

Not long into the first cups of coffee, the floodgates opened up. The three of us commiserated over the enormity of single motherhood, suddenly thrust upon us. The sadness within our kids that manifested at times in anger, and other times in solitude that we moms just couldn't penetrate. The abject loneliness of reaching across the bed in the middle of the night to find it still empty and cold, void of any cozy cuddling, any spontaneous passion. The insensitive acquaintances or co-workers who ignorantly insisted that "It's been (*fill in the blank*) weeks or months. Isn't it time you moved on?" The inability to accept the new mantle that hung around our necks, "widow."

Perhaps because we both had daughters or perhaps due to some peculiar bit of chemistry that neither of us could identify, Kathy and I soon forged a particularly fast friendship. When I would find myself overcome by life, weeping inconsolably after finally getting the last of the girls down to sleep for the night, or thinking I'd lost my mind when I just wanted to run away from the relentless responsibilities of my kids, Kathy understood. When one of us would collapse on the couch at night exhausted by handling alone all the endless parenting duties...beginning first thing in the morning with battles over teeth brushing and hair combing and ending at night with "please just go to sleep" pleadings...somehow the other always seemed to sense that a phone call to our buddy was needed. When one of us needed to be talked down off an emotional cliff, the other was miraculously in a better place in that moment and we'd often end that lifeline phone call laughing or at least calmer and better equipped to tackle another day.

Together, Kathy and I, often with our six girls in tow, navigated a lot of crazy experiences, some brand-new, others new to us now that we were single mothers, and they often involved travel. Our first road trip together, and perhaps winner of the oddest excursion award, was a trip to the Northwoods of Wisconsin and something called Beef-A-Rama. Held the last weekend of September every year in tiny Minocqua, it was, as the name implies, a celebration of all things beef, from an annual Rump Roast Run to a parade with cow-themed costumes to a Beef Eating Contest and something frighteningly called the Cow Pie Plop. Kathy had friends who regularly celebrated this curious family camping experience up north, and she thought it might be fun to join in their tradition, but she didn't want to plunge in alone. So she convinced me to explore this beef-camaraderie with her, promising a warm cabin (no tent, thank you), s'mores by the campfire, and even a tasty brandy slush or two or three once all of our girls were safely tucked into bed for the night.

In the months and years that followed, there were many more adventures with Kathy and me and our girls. We explored beautiful Door County in northeast Wisconsin from a quaint cabin on the shores of Lake Michigan. Our girls delighted in family dinner nights together where they would share the latest additions to their Beanie Baby collections. We took the first of what would become a tradition of annual trips to Florida for spring break, burying plastic treat-filled Easter eggs in the sand for our kiddos to find, luxuriating in the hotel pool and even having to drag my unwilling toddler Colleen out of the hot tub in 90-degree Florida heat. To this day, I'll never understand why that double whammy of extra heat and humidity was so attractive to a three-year-old.

The experiences Kathy and I shared over the years since our first, improbable meeting, did not always center on our kids. Our husbands' untimely deaths had rendered us much more than single moms. We were now, suddenly, and unwillingly thrust back into a world we had both left years before. Single. Period. No longer one half of a couple in a society very much shaped on coupledom.

Some married friends whom Steve and I had socialized with regularly suddenly grew distant. Party and dinner invitations fell off and it made me sad and confused at first, and then angry. I hadn't changed as a person, so why was it that I was no longer considered a valuable component of our previous social circle? One hypothesis offered by a well-meaning friend, one who had not abandoned me, was that a few of the female halves of these former couple friendships now perceived me as some sort of threat. A forty-one-year-old, reasonably attractive, intelligent single woman was not welcome in their circle for fear of what, competition? That I might now hit on their husbands or they on me? It was a ludicrous idea, yet the reality of this forced isolation seemed to explain the cold shoulders turned on me from these once-and-no-longer friends. I might have rejected this explanation were it not for the fact that I heard similar stories from Kathy and other widow friends, expressed with a similar degree of disbelief and upset.

In some sense, this social shutdown worked out for the best. Kathy and I decided it was time to find new friends willing to accept us in our current social strata. Not surprisingly, other young widows (we nicknamed ourselves the Ws) became a great resource for this. Cheryl, whom I had met at that first coffee with Kathy, and another friend of hers who had lost her husband to cancer made for a nice foursome. Together we enjoyed many child-free nights out...dinners, theater, often a nice bottle of wine. The social awkwardness of being identified as a widow was never an elephant in the room in this company. No longer was I moving in this world of young widowhood alone. It wasn't a case of I, but we. It was refreshing, and delightful, and restorative.

When our mutual funeral home director first suggested these two young widows should get together, neither Kathy nor I anticipated the exceptional, years-long bond that would result.

CHAPTER TWELVE

DATING

"We must be the architect of our lives after loss."

Author unknown

"So how do you girls know each other?"

First off, don't call us girls. Kathy and I were both in our forties. Our singles' bar radar immediately kicked into gear. This awkward small talk was clearly going nowhere and their lame inquiry gave us the perfect out.

"Our funeral home director introduced us," we responded without missing a beat.

Talk about a conversation-ender. Unsure of what to say next, our two new friends, sufficiently flustered, quickly excused themselves. Kathy and I were becoming pretty adept at extricating ourselves from such unpromising bar scenes. And besides, it was usually far more interesting just talking to each other, sharing some well-deserved adult time away from the kids.

Now, new girlfriends were one thing. It took many, many months after Steve died before I began to entertain

99

the prospect of expanding my world of new friends to include the opposite sex. The idea of actually dating again was weird, even a little frightening. I still felt married. Steve and I had supported each other as we grew our fresh-out-of-college jobs into successful careers that had once been mere dreams. We had struggled to find parenthood and then, finding the right formula four times over, delighted in sharing our children's achievements, large and small. All of this had allowed our connection as a couple over seventeen years, almost two decades when you count our courtship, to deepen and grow. How could I not still feel married?

But as each additional day passed without Steve, the aloneness was growing, gaping, and becoming more real, more present. The lack of a partner's loving caress or simple kiss, the physical and spiritual bond between man and woman, was achingly absent, particularly as I dealt with a cancer scare and the enormity of raising my daughters singlehandedly. And as another week, and month, and year slipped off the calendar, that emotional crevasse widened.

I do recall a sudden realization, probably a year and a half after Steve's death, when I awoke to a bright, sunny morning and decided in that moment, with no conscious forethought, that it was time to take off my wedding ring. I'm not sure what triggered this decision but it was definitive, even defining. I no longer had the presence, and comfort, and challenge, and joy of Steve in my life. I was no longer married. Steve was not by my side, had not been for many agonizing months, and the gold and diamond testament to that partnership made me feel almost like an imposter. Not by choice, but in a very real sense, Steve had abandoned me. So the ring came off and was lovingly tucked away into my jewelry box to be resurrected sometime far down the road when it might hold some special significance to one or more of my daughters.

That decision opened up a new world, one that I didn't even know I was seeking, if indeed I was. I had not abandoned my wedding ring with the intention of enhancing my prospects in the dating world. In fact, I still wrestled with an odd sense of guilt that in going out with another man I would somehow be cheating on my husband. This idea was ludicrous of course. Steve had been gone for months and months. But the heart and the brain often fall out of step with one another, and this "still married" conundrum certainly reflected that.

Not that I was looking to replace Steve, not in any conceivable way. Even the possibility of ever marrying again had not occurred to me. Yet, the concept of some new man in my life who might find me interesting and even desirable started to take hold, ever so cautiously. At the same time, the mere thought of re-entering the single world was puzzling, and peculiar, and a little frightening after nearly two decades of courtship and marriage to one man.

Perhaps not surprisingly, Kathy, on the same trajectory as me in terms of when we had lost our husbands, was beginning to consider this new singledom too, and together we decided to explore what we might do with it. So far removed from the dating scene, neither of us was really sure where to begin, or even what the world of dating looked like for two people well past their teenage and early twenties years when we had last been in the market, so to speak.

Our first forays into this new scene were laughable. I had heard of the group Parents Without Partners. Just by the name alone, it sounded like it could be a good, safe place to start our re-entry. The local PWP group held regular monthly meetings and social events and it seemed like that might be a less intimidating way of dipping our toes into the dating pool than hitting the bar scene, decades out of practice. So Kathy and I thought we'd give it a try.

I convinced my sister-in-law Cindy, recently divorced, to join us. Strength in numbers felt right. Or so we thought. It soon became clear that we were out of our element. As we pulled up to the address for this monthly Parents Without Partners meeting we found ourselves in the parking lot of a bowling alley.

"Are you sure you've got the right address?" Kathy asked with a hint of trepidation.

"That's what it says in the ad," I responded, dutifully double-checking the small piece of paper in my hand.

"Well, we've come this far," Cindy offered, "we might as well go in."

Our entree into this new social singledom was greeted by a loud, slightly sticky, beer-soaked ambiance with no clear indication of any "meeting" other than pins meeting their demise at the end of 15-pound orbs. But, good single soldiers that we were, we dutifully marched up to the stinky shoe rental counter.

"We're here for a Parents Without Partners meeting," I shouted to the disinterested teenage boy behind the counter. "Are we in the right place?"

"Yeah, it's upstairs," he said dismissing these three forty-something ladies in our semblance of date-night makeup off to a nearby stairwell.

Our greeting at the top of the stairs was not much more promising. A disinterested middle age guy at a card table in the entryway to the meeting room barely managed to tear himself away from his conversation with another PWP member when we approached. He unceremoniously handed us "Hello My Name Is..." stickers and precious little else in terms of information about what the night held in store. Opting not to partake of the grocery store cheese and crackers tray, and absent a more enthusiastic greeting by any of the handful of others in attendance, we quickly and simultaneously came to the same conclusion. PWP was not what we were looking for. A glass of wine among friends far away from this setting would be a much more interesting and beneficial use of our rare girls' night out. We peeled off our sticky name tags even before we hit the door to the parking lot.

That was just round one of what would become a series of trial-and-error experiences. Kathy had a sister-in-law widowed several years earlier who'd recently married a really nice guy she'd met at a singles' night at a local hotel bar.

"That worked for Grace, so why not for us?" Kathy had suggested.

The tiny basement bar lit mostly by neon should have been a tip off. I think we stuck it out for two drinks, only because there was a two-drink minimum, and deftly avoided the few leering gents who tried to catch our attention.

Then there were any number of new restaurants, and bars, and even local theatre companies trying to attract an audience of single baby boomers. Or perhaps they'd always been seeking that market but we were not aware of it until now. Kathy and I gamely explored our options, growing increasingly less optimistic about our chances of meeting a new Mr. Right, but figuring, if nothing else, it was a night out. A night of adult conversation. A temporary reprieve from the world of parent-teacher conferences, hosting 'tween birthday parties for our girls and cheerleading their many youth sporting events. It wasn't that we didn't enjoy all our kids' many activities. It was just that we began to crave a socialness that didn't center exclusively around adolescents.

The internet presented an alternative to the bars, a more anonymous way of meeting and screening candidates. Of course, online dating also had its own pitfalls and the nagging concern that a person's profile might be nothing more than smoke and mirrors. Still, it seemed to give me a little more control over who I might choose to communicate with and whether or not anything more than an email or two was worth the risk of a face-to-face encounter. It became an interesting late-night hobby, sorting through suggested matches and seeing if anyone had found my personal story worthy of further pursuit. The few guys that I decided to actually meet after our online introduction made me soon realize that Match.com was not the answer for me. Perhaps not outright fiascos, but most of these episodes quickly resulted in one or both of us anxious to end the date and say adieu.

Connections to and through old friends was yet another option that I pursued. These connections seemed a little less risky as they carried a known history or at least the recommendation of a well-meaning matchmaker friend. This resulted in a few pleasant short-term liaisons, intermixed with some near-disasters. I began to wonder why I even considered dating some of these prospects when they would not have been anyone who would have appealed to me in an earlier time. Why now? Was I so desperate?

What I came to appreciate was that it was perfectly natural to want companionship, on my own terms, in my own timeline. While I half expected Steve's family or friends to question my decision to date again, they did not, at least not that they ever expressed to me. The ones who did question that decision big time was my children.

Talk about complicated. Despite my assurances that I was in no way interested in replacing their father who was unique and special to us all, my girls refused to see my dating as anything else. They insisted that I was being "disloyal to Daddy," and much as I tried not to listen to such talk, my own inner qualms about still feeling married didn't help matters. Despite me putting my foot down and insisting that I had a right to happiness again, my kids were not about to give up so easily.

To varying degrees, they made it awkward and uncomfortable for me to have a guy show up at my doorstep, no matter how nice or kind or friendly he might be. Many times my date was greeted with outright rudeness that took on many forms. There were cold glares, disappearing acts where they'd avoid meeting the gentleman in question at all, and stubborn refusals to even answer innocent, well-meaning attempts to engage them in conversation. And good luck to any guy who mustered the fortitude to put up with my children's bad behavior more than once in order to see me again.

After a few failed attempts to introduce a date to my daughters and far too many apologies for their ill behavior that started date night off on shaky ground, I decided it was best to avoid these "meet my children" encounters all together. The early dating process was complicated enough. It seemed more fair to give a new relationship a chance rather than sabotage it before it barely got off the ground. If I were to get serious about a guy, I could address the family meeting inevitability down the road.

Eventually that did happen. Twice actually. The first was a guy who I knew casually, having briefly worked together years before. A chance run-in about six years into widowhood evolved into a four-year relationship with a kind man who valiantly put up with whatever my kids threw at him because he was so determined to be with me. He became a wonderful lifelong friend, despite our eventual decision that a long-term romantic commitment was not in the cards, kids or no kids.

In the five years that followed, I had become quite comfortable with my unattached status and the life that I had re-built fifteen years after Steve's death. Work was going great. My girls, now well into college and careers, seemed on their way to successes of their own. Not to say my job as a single parent was done, but the constant daily mothering demands of their young lives was now behind me. I had nurtured a great social circle of old and newer friends and it didn't feel like the idea of a new life partner was as much of a focus anymore. There were occasional dates, of course, but I was happy and perhaps less willing to spend time on any liaisons that I felt held no promise.

Then, out of the blue, an old co-worker, Kathleen, asked if I'd ever be interested in being set up. Her husband, a sportswriter, had a single friend who seemed to share a lot of my interests. They both thought it would be an interesting match.

"You like baseball and you're both writers," Kathleen offered. "He writes for the Milwaukee Brewers. Seems like a natural?"

"I've never been on a blind date in all of my fifty-six years," I told her.

Still, I had to admit she had me intrigued. Then when she insisted she and her husband would ease my discomfort by joining this prospective suitor and me for our first meeting over dinner, I thought I had nothing to lose.

"What the heck," I said. "If he's game, so am I."

When date night arrived, Kathleen kindly offered to pick me up so I wouldn't have to venture into the restaurant alone. The guys were saving a table at a neighborhood Italian restaurant, a very comfortable and appropriate choice since Larry and I also share Italian heritage, though his, he quickly pointed out, was purebred. With my twenty-five percent Italian amply mixed with plenty of Irish, at least there was some commonality, some basis for friendly conversation.

It turned out Larry and I shared many interests and similar background experiences. Writing, he a former university professor and published author of several baseball-themed books, and me, a journalist by profession, was an obvious one. But we soon discovered that we had both traveled a lot and wanted to do more exploring around the world. And we fostered a fierce love of the game of baseball, although we agreed to respectfully disagree on who's team was best, my beloved Detroit Tigers or one of their nemeses, his daunting Boston Red Sox.

A tentative, but mutually felt spark was lit over that first dinner and we soon fell into a solid and loving romance and friendship. Larry was a good cook, and he enjoyed making me homemade dinners, so those became a delightful mainstay of our relationship, as did Sunday mornings with the *New York Times* crossword puzzle. We enjoyed great movies, new, old, and often Italian, and planning and then executing a variety of travel experiences, across the US and to Europe.

Larry was ten years older than me and had recently retired as a university professor, while I was still working very much full time. Despite his almost unlimited availability compared to mine, we managed several trips to Italy and Sicily over the years. We found our way to Europe and a river cruise on the Rhine, visiting castles and other historical sites reminiscent of World War II as we made our way to Amsterdam, pinballing between France and Germany. He introduced me to his beloved New England, to Cooperstown, to wine country in California.

Larry, to his credit, found so much value in our love for one another that he, not always happily but resignedly, put up with much anger, resentment, and mistrust from my daughters in order to continue seeing me. And I determined that this was a relationship worth fighting for. I had to believe that my girls would eventually come around, if only for the passage of time. Larry wasn't going away. I wasn't going to push him away. We all needed to deal with that reality however it developed going forward.

It took overcoming a lot of hurdles to get there, but visiting the Netherlands with my beau Larry was well worth it.

CHAPTER THIRTEEN

THE MANY FIRSTS

"What lies behind you and what lies in front
of you pales in comparison to what lies inside
of you."

Ralph Waldo Emerson, author

"Oh Christmas tree, oh Christmas tree, I love my mom and
daddy," my innocent three-year-old crooned a cappella as
I tucked her into bed. I had been unable to muster up the
energy or the will to provide her with our nighttime ritual of
a book, a song, and a prayer. So Colleen, trying to be helpful,
took over as only she could.

Perhaps it was the magical glow of the holidays or
her tender age, but, in that moment, my little Colleen was
somehow oblivious to the reality of her dad's death just
two months earlier. With every song on the radio, every ad
on the TV, we were being blindsided with our first "first,"
our first Christmas without Dad. Oh, how I wished I could
capture some of that tender, innocent oblivion for myself.

Like boarding some colossal roller coaster, strapping in
for the ride ahead, and then climbing up that first insanely

high, terrorizing loop, navigating grief over the years after Steve died provoked intense fear, uncertainty, and a sometimes stomach-churning wave of emotions. Often the anticipation of some new first was worse than the actuality of it. But not always.

Our first Christmas post-Steve came barely two months after the funeral. I had always loved Christmastime. I couldn't wait to put up decorations inside and out, an elaborate mission that took me weeks to perfect each year. Even when artificial trees became the accepted standard, I would only agree to one if I could also have my real tree. No matter if that meant doubling the time and work of decorating. There was just no replacing the tradition of hunting down the perfect tree. Struggling to get it to stand soldier-like in the front window without toppling over and smashing all the ornaments so carefully hung. Turning last year's tangle of lights into a beautiful halo of color. The scent of live pine as we sat back to admire our handiwork with a crackling fire in the nearby fireplace. When it came to wrapping presents, I coyly coveted the "they're too pretty to open" comments. Every year, at least before children came along, I would make handmade ornaments for all the relatives and delight in their expectation of this new year's additions. And I was infamous, some would say annoyingly so, at playing Christmas carols non-stop from the first stroke of Thanksgiving through New Years'.

Sharing the holidays each year with Steve, who for years played part-time Santa at the local mall, increased the joy of the season manyfold. Early in our relationship we often Christmas-caroled with friends, structured full evenings around re-connecting with old college and high school buddies, and delighted in learning about the traditions that had guided each of our large extended families for generations. This included the orange Jell-O mold, always in the shape of a star, that made a mandatory appearance at Christmas dinner on the Cullen side. This was certainly not because it was some culinary delight, but because Cullen family history dictated that you just couldn't have Christmas without it, whether or not any scoop of it ever made it onto your plate. We learned to cross-country ski together when enough pre-Christmas snow had fallen to make that possible in Milwaukee if a trip to the north woods just couldn't materialize. And I learned that St. Nicholas always filled Christmas stockings on the night of December 5th, at least in Wisconsin. In my hometown of Detroit, my sisters and I tried tacking up socks on the fireplace mantle on Christmas Eve, ever hopeful that Santa would fill them, but after awakening multiple Christmas mornings to the same, empty socks, we came to accept that Santa, at least in Michigan, preferred leaving his gifts under the tree.

Steve and I had many Christmas Eve and Christmas Day traditions to share with both of our extended families, first in Milwaukee, then later in Detroit, a long car ride away in sometimes hazardous winter weather. Every one of those four hundred miles was worth the warm family reunion that always awaited, at least it was for me. My dear Steve would fire up for this annual trek every year, not because he loved all my family's traditions and personalities necessarily, but because he loved me. And, of course, the magic of Christmas was compounded exponentially as Steve and I discovered it anew through the eyes of our four little girls.

Perhaps that's why that first Christmas without Steve was so horrific. I couldn't turn on the radio or read the paper or drive anywhere without being bombarded by endless reminders of the joy that was so vacant in my own life. And forget the mall. I was aware that gifts ought to be purchased, but the mere thought of going anywhere near these tinseled, red-bowed, deck-the-halls establishments paralyzed me. Christmas decorations that I once was so passionate about sat in storage, and were it not for my sister, Joan, and other relatives, I'm pretty sure not even a Christmas tree would have made an appearance that year. While my head told me I needed to somehow preserve the spirit of Christmas for my young daughters, the oldest of whom was only nine, I couldn't muster the will or the energy. I just didn't care. In Steve's absence, Christmas had become a chore, something to be endured until it passed.

Of course, with time, the paralysis that marked that first Christmas and so many other firsts in our post-Steve lives eventually began to dissipate or be replaced by other often conflicting emotions. The intense pride I would feel as each of my daughters made their first communions or sang a solo in the spring concert or graduated from grade school, and then high school, and college was always coupled with a sadness that their dad was not there to appreciate those wonderful moments. His unabashed joy at sharing the girls' simplest accomplishments, from taking their first steps, to making it through their first day at school each fall, to losing a first tooth was noticeably absent, certainly to me, and I suspect to our girls, too, as each new "first" came our way.

And not every of these challenging moments in time was mitigated by what was otherwise a positive life event. My girls' high school had an annual Father/Daughter dance that I absolutely dreaded for them as they reached freshman year. The school made so much of this event in the weeks leading up to the big night, oblivious to any students whose dads couldn't or wouldn't be able to attend, that it was like pouring salt in an open wound. Peer pressure or just the desire not to be the odd-girl-out inevitably swept up each of my girls when they first encountered this school tradition, like it or not. I put on a brave face as I helped the girls dress up and primp for the dance, and wished them a fun time with whatever well-meaning stand-in dad they had chosen to be their date for the night, all the time silently wishing I could protect them from what, in my mind, would be an inevitable disappointment. Ultimately it took only one or two of these dances and my girls each discovered on their own what I had wanted to shield them from, the overwhelming sadness and loneliness that this night inevitably represented.

Molly put it simply, "I know I went to father/daughter once. It was just super awkward."

Kathleen's take was a bit deeper. "I think it's hard because developmentally you want to be with your peers," Kathleen admitted. "And although I was glad I saw it, it's not something I would recommend doing."

Steve's absence was palpable.

My own insecurities in the role of only parent also presented many challenges. I remember the night Annie, then twelve, got a phone call she'd been anxiously anticipating. The news wasn't good. She did not make the select soccer team, a particularly bitter pill since most of her current team, including her coach, was moving on to select. I couldn't help wondering if Steve, ever the sports enthusiast, had been there to cheer her on from the sidelines or perhaps even help out as coach, she might have had more inspired play.

Annie was pretty matter-of-fact about the situation.

"I don't think I ever felt like 'I wish my dad was coaching' because I always had coaches that I liked," she told me later. So maybe I worried too much.

Still, I felt so inadequate, not just because my own knowledge of soccer rendered me incapable of delivering any meaningful playing tips, but more so as her mother, that I couldn't seem to find the right words to ignite her inner fire when a game she loved so much was on the line. I hated having to handle this parenting thing alone. It was so unfair to our girls. They deserved so much more.

Other firsts brought more bittersweet moments. Annie got her master's degree, helping to launch her profession as an athletic trainer. She was our eldest. The first to pursue graduate school. Despite the anxiety attacks that still dogged her following Steve's death, she had persevered and become a determined and focused young woman ready to take on life.

Then there was Kathleen, who became an independent world traveler starting in high school, when she figured out how to finance a school science excursion to Hawaii. That was followed in her twenties with explorations of China, South America, Australia, New Zealand, and Norway. In fact, she got herself to every continent but Antarctica before the age of thirty, all while completing undergraduate and degrees. When we climbed Table Mountain together in Capetown, South Africa, I remember marveling, certainly at the whole southern hemisphere stretched out before us, but even more so at the confident, compassionate, and adventurous young woman my daughter had become.

Molly's pinning ceremony signifying she had officially become a registered nurse was one I hated to attend as a single parent. Even from an early age, Steve and I had recognized the potential in this kid with her falling-off-a-log-easy smarts. While it took three universities and a number of fits and starts along the way, Molly had finally achieved the first step in a promising medical career. She was radiant and confident as she was honored for her hard-won accomplishment.

Colleen's tenacity and ambition would have been very close to Steve's heart. She volunteered for many political campaigns and social causes throughout college, using those experiences to help convince the prestigious Georgetown University Law School to admit her. Graduating with distinction was icing on the cake.

The physical absence of Steve in these life events was always felt, but I comforted myself with the belief that somehow, he would have, and maybe still could, appreciate these moments too, equally proud of all our daughters had become and all that lay ahead.

While the passage of time certainly helped ease the frequency and blunted some of the impact of these many firsts, it never resolved them or made them disappear altogether, a tribute to the enormity of the person, the personality whose loss I was grieving. Even years out from Steve's sudden death I would sometimes find myself gob-smacked by grief. Not surprisingly, many of these were momentous times for my family and me.

Having my would-be sons-in-law ask to marry my daughters was certainly bittersweet. While I was happy for each daughter and the life she was so excited to build with her partner, I also felt terribly ill-prepared in that moment. Being somewhat traditional, I had always thought it would be Steve sizing up the young suitor and asking hard questions to make sure he was worthy of our daughter. Instead, I found myself almost tongue-tied, stalling for time as I tried to measure up to the weightiness of the task before me.

Walking each of my daughters down the aisle on their wedding days brought another tangle of emotions. The outward expression of these emotions varied from one wedding to the next depending on the length of the aisle or the number of distractions at procession time. In one case, the not quite two-year-old grandson I had to snag to keep from running away offered some comic relief. With the squirming grandson in one arm and the bride on the other, I didn't have time to dwell on who was not there with us that day. In the case of my other daughters' weddings, I didn't have that blessed distraction. Many a tear was choked back and quite a few escaped. Thank goodness for waterproof mascara.

My first intercontinental adventure after Steve died was visiting Kathleen in Cape Town, South Africa where she was studying and teaching for a semester in college. This was a trip of a lifetime in so many respects.

Colleen's graduation with distinction from Georgetown
University Law School was one of many standout,
bittersweet moments I encountered as a single parent.

Chapter Fourteen

CANCER

"So before I save someone else, I've got to save myself."

Ed Sheeran, lyrics from "Save Myself"

"You have cancer."

Those three words turned my world upside down and shook me to my soul. I didn't feel sick. I had no family history or poor lifestyle to blame. I hadn't felt this frightened, this vulnerable since that phone call six years earlier when I discovered that Steve had inexplicably died, alone in his hotel room miles from home.

When I became a suddenly single parent, it was in many ways like becoming a parent for the very first time. No one is ever prepared for the responsibility and endless worries over whether you are performing well enough to properly advance this young life that's been entrusted to you. And even though there are plenty of books on the subject and countless well-meaning friends or relatives who offer advice, there really is no one with all the right answers to the endless questions that new parents face, moment by moment, day by day, year by year. It is a bit of a trial and error experience backed by daily prayers that you don't screw things up too badly.

In my case, I had a loving partner in this monumental task. Steve, like me, had the DNA invested in our growing family and the shared determination that we could master, or at least not totally botch, this concept of parenting. Together, we would shoulder the responsibility for turning four newborns into successful, accomplished, well-rounded young women someday. That was the plan, crafted and articulated with so much care. And then, in an instant, that plan went horribly, irretrievably wrong, veering off course like a race car that suddenly experiences a total brake failure while flying around the final turn into the home stretch. My partner on this journey was stripped from my life with no forewarning. There was no chance to explore his opinions on what sports our girls might play, if they should play them at all, or where they would go to high school, how best to interrogate first boyfriends, or what to tell them about sex, and love, and commitment, and so, so much more.

The enormity of handling every parenting role and life decision singlehandedly evoked a hyper-vigilance in me, as my girls would attest. They were already dealing with the gaping emotional wounds left by their dad's death. I subconsciously determined that I would do anything and everything in my power to make up for those gaps. I guess I thought that becoming Wonder-Mother would somehow ease their loss, that my mission in this new role of single parent was to answer every question, attend every event, help with every test preparation or school project, volunteer to be Girl Scout leader, you name it.

What I didn't see, in fact, what I was totally blind to, was that I was no superhero, and in all my efforts to become one, I was actually doing a disservice to my girls. As Ed Sheeran so eloquently writes in his song "Save Myself," I had to learn that "before I save someone else, I've got to save myself." My five sisters harped this at me relentlessly, if not quite as melodically as singer/songwriter Sheeran.

"If you get sick, how's that going to go for the girls?" they would tell me.

Slowly I started to heed this sage advice. Hard as it was for me to find a spare half-hour in my day and a willing babysitter available at the same time, I got back into running. The routine of uncounted steps and an uncluttered mind, even for just those few moments, became a welcome form of therapy. With no one to tug at me literally or emotionally for those brief respites, I was gifting myself with the power to head back into the single parenting fray again, with renewed energy to deal with whatever awaited.

And then came 2001 and the start of an odyssey that had nothing to do with Stanley Kubrick's film masterpiece. It was nonetheless a huge, daunting journey of its own that changed the trajectory of our family in multiple ways. I had been to the doctor for the annual mammogram that we women endure in the interest of self-care and self-preservation, two motivators that had become more top of mind now that I was the lone parent of four adolescent and young teenage girls. I had survived this vaguely humiliating, breast-squishing, contortionist dance with the mammography machine every year since I turned forty. Seven years into this annual obligation, it was a resigned "you need to do this for your health" grin-and-bear-it approach that drove with me to the hospital that crisp December day. It would soon be over...put away for another mammogram, another day, another year.

When the doctor's office called the next afternoon, the calm and very professional nurse told me "the radiologist just needs a second look." She was reassuring. This was no big deal. Really just a precaution. The idea of a second breast exam, this time an ultrasound, seemed more of an inconvenience, one more thing to find time for between work and multiple family commitments. I hadn't felt any changes in my breasts. I was strong and healthy. Why worry?

Round two happened the next afternoon, followed immediately by a needle biopsy and then, the following day with a brief appointment with a grey-haired surgeon I had never met and soon choose not to remember by name.

"You have breast cancer, Mrs. Cullen," he said with a clinical accuracy veiled in a remarkable lack of empathy. And then he shook my hand. Had I just won the lottery? I was dumfounded.

"The next step will be a lumpectomy so we can determine the best course of treatment. I'd recommend a mastectomy, but we can talk about your options later," he said with all the compassion of a turnip. "But let's not get ahead of ourselves," he said coldly. "First, the lumpectomy. You can schedule this with the nurse on your way out."

Summarily dismissed, and in a total state of shock, I literally didn't know what to do next. The "C" word sent my mind reeling, my emotions overcome by a ten-thousand pound elephant of fear. And the questions. So many questions. Should I wander the shopping mall that housed the surgeon's office to try to compose myself? Surely I couldn't go home. Am I going to die? What will this news do to my daughters, still in so many ways dealing with the loss of their father just six years earlier? How could I possibly deliver the words that would place their remaining parent, this outwardly strong, invincible persona of Mom in such jeopardy?

I had driven myself to this appointment, not expecting any sort of monumental news, and it didn't occur to me to call anyone in that moment. So, unable to face the tsunami of worries and the answerless questions before me, I opted for the short drive to the grocery store as a curious but anonymous source of refuge. It was an out-of-body experience, watching my devastated-self wander alone up and down the aisles, trying to keep the tears in check so as not to scare off other shoppers, as I randomly placed meaningless items of food into a cart.

The one thing I couldn't purchase was time. Ultimately, I knew I had to go home and face the reality of my diagnosis. I had to admit not just to myself, but to my daughters, that life had taken yet another jagged turn. I steeled myself for the inevitable tears, anxiety, and uncertainty that lie ahead. I had to be the brave face. The calm in the storm. Yet inside I was anything but.

The reactions of my girls were as unique as each of their personalities. The younger girls seemed to buy my contrived calm, that this was likely just a matter of a minor surgery and some follow up treatments. Kathleen, ever the care-taker, was worried about me and wanted to be helpful in any way possible. Then there was Annie, my eldest, who got very quiet and put up a stoic front that I knew from experience masked the sheer terror she held inside. There was a little bit of anger, too.

"Why didn't you tell us what all these doctor appointments were about, Mom," Annie, now a sophomore in high school, wanted to know. She had stumbled across the paperwork on the kitchen counter that indicated I had had a biopsy. "Did you think we were stupid, that we didn't know something was up?"

In the weeks that followed, there was a litany of new and frightening experiences. The first order of business was finding a new surgeon, one who cared about me as a person and not just as a tumor. I reached out to a friend, a former colleague, who had become something of an advocate for women with breast cancer. She not only recommended someone she herself had used, but she made phone calls to his office to make sure this surgeon, very much in demand because of his compassion as much as his skill, would see me. Then there was another lumpectomy to be followed by eight weeks of daily radiation treatments.

Luckily, no chemotherapy was recommended because my cancer was found at an early stage. Still the radiation was bizarre and scary. Perhaps this whole cancer journey was more like "Space Odyssey" after all. It started with being introduced to "my" oncologist. The mere word oncologist screamed cancer patient to me. Then to think that I now had one specifically assigned to me was forcing me to accept the ugly reality. I had cancer.

My radiation journey began with a two-hour consultation to fit me with a customized plaster mold of my chest. Now that was an experience I hope never to have to endure again. As I recall, I had to lower my naked upper body face-down onto a gurney open to a vat of wet plaster below. Then I had to lay there for an interminable length of time until the mold fully dried around my chest and could be extracted intact from my skin. This device was supposed to ensure that day after day, week after week, I would assume the exact same position on the gurney to allow the intense bolts of radiation energy to be repeatedly focused on the cancerous cells in my left breast while damaging as few healthy, normal cells nearby as possible. Fun times.

My work was very understanding. I was able to put in regular hours every morning and then go to my radiation appointments at the same time each afternoon. That allowed plenty of time to get home to greet the girls after school. My oncologist even allowed me to temporarily suspend the treatments for a week about a month into the process so I could take the girls on a long-planned spring break trip to

Florida. It was a seamless transition into the life of cancer patient. At least I tried to make it appear that way.

Inside, the fears for my longevity festered, despite an optimistic prognosis. The thought of laying on that radiation table day after day while they zapped the offending breast and tried to keep those same rays from damaging my heart or lungs never failed to stir up my anxiety quotient. And I determined the side effects were mine to handle, and mine alone. No one else needed to hear that I tired more easily or that the skin of my left breast was so seared from the daily burning that I wanted to claw it off because it itched so badly. The good soldier marched on, still protecting her family from any signs of vulnerability.

I did try to crack that mask of invincibility once, sitting my daughters down for a family meeting about my diagnosis and wanting to answer any questions they might have about the likelihood that they, too, could be vulnerable to breast cancer in the future. I wanted to know what the girls were feeling, to see if I could calm their fears, ease their worries. It was a short meeting. Only Colleen, my youngest, later admitted she was terrorized though she never verbalized it at the time.

"I definitely thought you were going to die," she told me.

The other girls seemed somewhat disinterested and quickly wanted to move beyond any talk about their own health. Years later Molly told me the cancer seemed like no big deal.

"You never looked sick or seemed sick," she said. "It was scary obviously, because I only had one parent left, and my parent had a disease that we knew killed people, but you never made it seem like life was any different, really."

The older girls were a bit more aware of changes brought about by the cancer. There was a meal train by kind friends and neighbors so I didn't have to worry about making dinner during my treatments. And there were a lot of other offers of help, taking the girls to their various activities or running errands if I was too tired, that sort of thing. Kathleen, very wise for fourteen, certainly remembered that as a time when our family, perhaps subconsciously, pulled together and found strength in a difficult situation.

"Knowing that we had each other as sisters, but also connecting us to step up more, and appreciate you and our time together, is how I looked at it," Kathleen recounted.

Annie took heart in my insistence that everything was going to be fine.

"I think one of the first things you told the doctors was that you were a single mom with four kids," she told me. "So I think I felt reassured in what was going to happen."

Reassured and also willing to let me lean on her a bit as my eldest. When I was radiation-exhausted and didn't have the strength to argue with the little girls about taking a shower or doing their homework or getting to bed, Annie would step in, often without me even asking.

My sister, Pat, noticed my increasing reliance on Annie, almost to the point of co-parenting.

"I remember thinking she's too young for such major responsibility," Pat would later say. "But, in Steve's absence, I knew you oftentimes needed a sounding board as well as a shoulder and Annie was there."

It was true. While I tried not to unload too much onto my eldest daughter, there was a selfish comfort in knowing I wasn't facing this cancer journey totally alone.

Annie and I attending a wine tasting event in Cagli, Italy.
She successfully overcame many anxieties to join me as a
student advisor in my study abroad teaching experience.

Chapter Fifteen

GROWING BEYOND GRIEF

"If you don't see that growth is possible, you're not going to find it."

Sheryl Sandberg, author

"I need you to come down to campus, Mom," my college sophomore Kathleen nonchalantly offered in one of our weekly catch-up phone calls. "There's somebody I want you to meet."

When I tried to press her for details, Kathleen was non-committal. "Just meet me at the Union at two on Friday."

Not sure if I was about to meet some new beau or next semester's roommate, I did as instructed and drove to the campus in downtown Milwaukee. Soon I was sitting across the desk from a woman who Kathleen introduced as "the organizer of this great study-abroad program I'm going to do."

It seemed my twenty-year-old daughter was determined to go to Capetown, South Africa to teach underprivileged children while exploring the social and political history of this complicated land. So determined, in fact, that she had arranged this meeting so that the program director could answer all my questions and put to rest any fears or anxiety I might have about sending my naïve young daughter halfway around the world to a country known to me only as the home of apartheid, of enormous racial unrest.

I came out of that meeting onboard with Kathleen's grand design, but also with a surprising new appreciation of the strong, thoughtful, ambitious daughter I had raised. It was a moment that would come back to me many times in the years that followed, a moment of grace and growth that would provide clarity and inspiration as I took stock of my own life and how far I had come.

After six years of pulling my life back together in fits and starts following my cancer diagnosis, I was beginning to feel like I was back on somewhat solid ground. Physically, I was pretty healthy and active, and emotionally I allowed myself to believe that I was managing pretty well in this single parenting mode. I had figured out how to make sure my girls didn't miss out on activities they would have certainly experienced had their dad been around. Even if that meant all four of them playing soccer every spring and fall, with four different practice and game schedules all at different fields, I managed to pull it off, though maybe not with the level of attention to the play before me as I contemplated moving on to the next stop of the day. Despite all my hours at one match and another, and then another, I still hadn't quite mastered the concept of offsides. Still, I had learned to rely on my growing support network to help make all this happen. I had found ways to make my kids' lives full and mostly happy and even fun on a good day.

If it wasn't soccer, it was volleyball or basketball, or Girl Scouts, or sleepovers with friends. And, somehow, in the hectic pace of our daily lives, I had also managed to eke out a bit of "me" time, playing cards with friends once a month, grabbing a girl's lunch to catch up with my sister, Joan, or going out for a glass of wine or dinner with my best buddy, Kathy. There was even an occasional date here and there.

I have to admit that whole concept of dating again, of potentially finding some new significant other to share my life with, was a tricky puzzle. The total disruption of life as I had known it, and as I had envisioned its future pre-widowhood, pre-cancer, had again been thrown back to square one. My cancer diagnosis made me look at my own mortality and to question what was really important, what I really needed or wanted going forward. My ultimate goal had to be to be around to see my kids grow up. I questioned whether my haphazard pursuits into the world of dating were even worth the effort. I knew I didn't need a man to validate my existence or to somehow complete me, whatever that meant, and I wasn't even sure I wanted one.

Yet there was still this nagging sense that I might be missing something. Perhaps the gaping hole in my post-Steve existence might need filling with more beyond the endless activities that I performed each day before falling into bed exhausted, knowing that a similar crazy schedule awaited with the dawn. Perhaps I needed to reimagine my life beyond the current moment. My girls were not going to be so present in my daily life forever. They were already moving forward in new directions, getting ready for college, and future careers, and lives and families of their own. Didn't I deserve to do as much for myself? I was conflicted. I was still a tangle of emotions.

Ultimately it may have been the wisdom of my children that helped me appreciate, at least in part, some clues that were right in front of me. Not that they, at their young ages, would have been schooled in the psychology of loss, but they seemed to innately grasp the idea that positive change can result from adversity. One of these positivities was improved personal relationships.

My growing friendship with fellow-widow Kathy was a prime example. We shared the knowledge that we could tell each other anything and never fear judgement, because we were living full-tilt the particular challenges that being a widow and a single mom had placed on us. We were helping each other survive.

Our kids intuited the value of this unique bond perhaps before Kathy or I even fully recognized it ourselves. They encouraged us to go out together. Of course, they did have one ulterior motive. If Kathy and I were hanging out, they were smart enough to realize that might minimize the number of stray guys who would show up at our doorsteps for a date. But I also believe they witnessed the healing, and kindness, and actual joy that this friendship had brought to their mothers. Even at their young ages, they understood how valuable it was to us both, and ultimately to them, for us to reimagine our lives following our unspeakable loss.

This was about far more than resiliency and finding the strength and resources to soldier on. Not to knock resiliency, which had been a godsend particularly in the early years after losing my husband. Resiliency had helped me find the strength to put a simple, healthy meal on the table to feed four young kids when every fiber in my being just wanted to crawl into a hole. It had gotten me out of bed each day, usually still exhausted, and somehow helped me wrestle with the morning rituals of getting the kids off to school or day care, and then hauling myself into work, and being somehow productive.

This concept of daring to think that there was more out there for me than basic survival started to develop. I needed to give myself permission to think about my future and what it might look like. To reimagine my life and grow in the aftermath of death.

I later learned this new approach of mine actually had a name, post-traumatic growth. I was purposefully seeking ways to grow stronger, physically and emotionally, and to allow myself space for personal introspection. I was determined to find ways to better craft this life I'd been handed, not just to simply make it through each day.

Besides new relationships, post-traumatic growth expressed itself in other ways. I came to discover that Steve's loss, compounded by my bout with cancer, heightened my appreciation for things I might have once taken for granted. I began to make a conscious effort to at least try to live in the moment. To absorb the nuances of a sunny, spring day. To relish the unprompted hugs from a child or grandchild. To try to take stock every day of the blessings in my life.

I wasn't always successful at this. More than once I would find myself caught up in the chaos or clutter or noise that inevitably resulted from a big family gathering, and I'd find myself turning grumpy. In these moments, sometimes with a small admonishment from one of my daughters, I'd at least try to pull back from the edge, to hit the pause button and look at the beautiful panorama before me. How lucky was I to have a family that enjoyed sharing a meal or a Packer game or a birthday celebration with each other and with me. A sink full of dirty dishes was nothing to stress over.

Sweating the small stuff was also no longer a thing. Grudges were a meaningless waste of time. I became more willing to accept differences I might have with someone, particularly with someone close, and just let them go. I might grouse about the person or the issue at hand a bit before I let them go, but I came to realize that the fight of the moment wasn't worth the long-term loss of their friendship. Nothing was worth that. I had already endured one huge loss over which I had no control. If I could prevent another by reining in my reaction to minor squabbles, so much the better.

Another part of my growth since Steve's death was a combination of the physical and the spiritual. I established a regular routine of exercising. As I ran or walked or used the elliptical machine that a friend had kindly handed down to me, I would take stock of my life and my place in the world. I would pray for comfort for family or friends who had lost a loved one or who were ill or struggling in some way. I made a point of expressing gratitude for each of my kids, for my sisters and extended family, for dear friends, old and new. I tried to call up world or national events or disasters and remember the people impacted by them. These daily prayers became a calming influence, forcing me, at least in that moment, to turn off all the distractions that bombarded me between work and parenting and running a busy household. For at least thirty to forty minutes every day my mind needed to get lost in an exercise ritual so that I could completely appreciate the good in my life as well as the needs of others.

Finding the courage to grow in the face of grief, to imagine a new life far beyond what I had ever expected, was a concept that was put to the test in a big way thirteen years after Steve died. A university professor who attended my church had hired me decades earlier to teach a journalism class, which I did for three years until I reluctantly gave up the post due to the demands of my growing family. From that moment on, whenever I would see Bill at church, he would invariably try to convince me to come back to teaching. I always put him off.

"I'm too busy, Bill," was my usual comeback. "Between work and all the kids' activities, there just isn't time."

Later, after Steve's death, the response was similar. "Being a single mother is such hard work," I'd tell Bill. "I truly appreciate the offer, but I just can't imagine finding room in my life for anything more right now."

That didn't stop the inquiries. If dogged determination had a face, it would be Bill's. It was almost getting to the point where I would try to avoid running into him and replaying that same conversation yet again. But ultimately Bill said something that made me take notice.

"I'd really like you to help teach a multi-media journalism course this summer," Bill said. "But before you say no, I've got to tell you, it will be held in Italy."

"Italy?," I said, not sure I had heard him correctly.

"Yes, it's a month-long study abroad program for American college students. We're pairing up a journalism course with one on Italian language and culture, and you'd be perfect to teach the TV production component."

I had to admit I was intrigued. I had visited Italy once before and absolutely loved it. I told Bill I needed to give it some thought.

"I'm happy to provide more details," Bill said. "I just need to know fairly soon because the program is in June and we only have about five months to plan it."

This was a huge, exciting opportunity, that unleashed a torrent of doubts and fears in my mind. My older daughters were adults, done or soon to be done with college. But the younger two were not quite nineteen and just sixteen years old. This presented a more challenging situation. They were a bit beyond the age of needing babysitters, yet the idea of me being a world and multiple time zones away for an extended period of time required some creative thinking on my part. Was I being selfish to even entertain the possibility of going to Italy for five weeks in pursuit of something just for me? How could I ensure that my girls would be safe; that they would eat properly, get where they needed to go, or not throw crazy parties in mom's absence? Who would take care of the house, and the lawn, and even general cleaning, if I wasn't there to mind the store? Would any of my girls meticulously water my multitude of houseplants so they didn't all die in my absence? I had to admit I was a bit of a fanatic about this, but still, it was important to me.

Perhaps dealing with Steve's loss and the countless obstacles, developments, and complications that resulted from it finally paid a dividend. All the fits and starts of grief had helped me to grow personally as well as professionally. I had more confidence in my role as a mother as well as in my career and in my ability to offer some seasoned advice and counsel to college students looking to join the world of video journalism. I was actually seriously entertaining this crazy offer to pursue a dream job of teaching a study-abroad program in Italy, leaving my daughters to cope with life without me for the better part of June and into July. I gave Bill a call.

Half of the faculty and students in our 2012 Italian study abroad program for Marquette University. My dear friend and mentor, Bill Thorn, is in the center of the bottom row in front of me.

CHAPTER SIXTEEN

THE BICYCLE ACCIDENT

"Sometimes life throws us a curve ball.
It doesn't go the way we planned. All that
matters is how we handle it and the person
we become on the other side."

Karina Halle, author

It was July 3, 2010. I had just returned from a month living
and working in central Italy for the second summer in a row.
I had accepted the offer to teach multi-media storytelling to
American college kids in the Apennine mountains in tiny,
picturesque Cagli and equally blessed to have a generous
and understanding boss back home who was willing to
allow me leave to pursue this exceptional opportunity. But
living five weeks and a continent away from my kids with,
at best, sketchy internet service to connect me to their voices
and periodic updates was enough. I was glad to be home.
Glad to be back in the warm embrace of family, to catch up
on their lives face to face and assure myself that my girls had
survived just fine, even with me being a continent away for
an extended time. I was even glad even for the only slightly

jet-lagged return to work, to a job I loved. I was happy, confident, and excited to share my Italian experience with my co-workers and friends.

Looking to start this new grounding in my normal routine on a positive note, I decided to ride my bike into work that first day back. It was a 14-mile route mostly through bike paths and county parks from the west side of Milwaukee where I lived to my office downtown. At one point, about midway on my ride, I crossed through the parking lot of the Milwaukee Brewers baseball stadium, Miller Park, to connect with the Hank Aaron Bike Trail that would swiftly deliver me to my office with minimal traffic interference. It was a route I had taken numerous times over the years, though this was my first attempt that particular summer. Attempt, because this ride was unceremoniously and dangerously ended by a slim but sturdy cable stretched across the eastern driveway leading out of the stadium lot to the bike trail, apparently meant to discourage drivers from parking in the lot between Brewer homestands.

It was a perfect storm, a perfect catastrophe actually. I had not anticipated the wire barrier as it had never been there before. I was enjoying the heady downhill slope into downtown. And I was caught up in the warm, bright sunshine of a mid-summer morning. By the time I saw the cable, I was too close to swerve away and going way too fast to safely stop. I panicked. I grabbed the brakes, connecting only with the front pair which did a particularly efficient job of stopping my front tire instantly and sending me careening head-first over the handlebars onto the blacktopped pavement.

Of course, I instinctively tried to brace my fall, which may have protected my helmeted head from more serious damage than a mere concussion, but it did no favors to my wrists, both wrists. The cell phone that might have been used to call 9-1-1 was rendered useless by the fact that it was zippered into a backpack that my crippled arms couldn't have accessed if they tried. And the lower arm and wrist bones, badly broken and protruding nastily from both arms, would not have been able to manipulate the dialing of a phone even if it had landed right in front of me on the open ground. Combine that with a state of shock that set in almost instantaneously, and I was sunk. At 7:30 in the morning, the baseball stadium parking lot was hours away from any useful activity that might bring forward some good Samaritan, and the largely industrial Menomonee Valley that contained the ballfield was remote, almost desolate, sandwiched as it was between miles of train tracks on the north side and the Menomonee River to the south.

If I've learned anything in the process of losing a loved one, it is that grief is not linear. Just when you think you've mastered it and moved forward into your new reality, you get knocked down a peg or two. If ever I was getting too cocky about my ability to navigate my life single-handedly, here was yet another wakeup call, another lesson to be learned, quite literally the hard way. A higher power was definitely at play, reminding me that I was no wonder woman while providentially tossing me a lifeline.

At the moment of my accident, a lone car happened to pass by, a guy on his way to work, probably looking for a less-traveled path to avoid rush hour traffic. Not only did he witness what no one else was around to see or would have seen for hours, but he came to my help immediately, he and his training, miraculously, as an EMT.

"Don't you worry," I vaguely recall him telling me through the fog that was my brain in the moment. "I'll make sure they get you to the hospital right away."

This angel of a man got me stabilized and convinced me that, as bad as I was hurting, or not hurting…I couldn't feel my hands...that I would be ok. He called 9-1-1 and helped the emergency crew that arrived place me carefully in the back of the ambulance with minimal disruption to my broken body. To say that he was a life-saver doesn't do him justice.

Shock and my concussion probably saved me from remembering much about the trip to the hospital or the initial assessment of my injuries in the emergency room. Clearly both wrists were badly broken and there were plenty of scrapes, bruises, and bloody road rash from my fall. My face had taken some of the brunt, too, including a front tooth that had lost the fight with the blacktop. There was an emergency surgery to stabilize my arms. A second, more elaborate surgery would follow the next day, to fine tune the repositioning of bones, tendons, and nerves into what was hoped would return both wrists to some semblance of their former abilities after considerable healing and months of physical therapy.

Life immediately after the bike episode was almost surreal. In order to put my wrists back together and keep them immobile so they could heal, the surgeon had screwed eight-inch-long stabilizer bars into the bones of both lower arms. Yep. Screws. Metal screws. Kind of like the kind you might pick up at the local hardware store, just a sterilized version to meet this particular need. With these lovely metal appendages, supplemented by dual slings to hold them away from my sides so blood would continue flowing into my hands, I looked like some version of Frankenstein.

And the maintenance on these contraptions anchored into my hands and the radius bones of my lower arms was not for the faint of heart. Three times a day one of my daughters or sisters drew the unlucky short straw and had to meticulously swab around each screw with rubbing alcohol on a Q-tip. This served a dual purpose. The most obvious goal was to keep the wounds clean and free from infection.

142

But there was also the matter of lubrication to make sure those same screws didn't take up permanent residence in my arms. After eight weeks of healing, the screws would need to be untwisted, with a very pedestrian Black & Decker drill mind you, to remove the metal stabilizer bars.

Aside from the wound care, my needs were many. Luckily, there was a rush of kind souls wanting to help in any way they could the moment I got home from the hospital. They brought wonderful, delicious meals, and there was never a shortage of folks to feed them to me, rendered as I was almost infantile with no use of my arms or hands. An army of relatives, neighbors, and friends lined up to take care of the house, too, well beyond basic maintenance which would have been more than enough. They emptied out and restocked my refrigerator, cleaned and organized my freezer, weeded my gardens and manicured the lawn. They handled all my laundry, making sure I was comfortable in clean sheets and fluffy towels. One neighbor even gifted me with special voice-activated computer software so I could "speak" email updates to my family and work friends.

My relatively new beau – we'd only been seeing each other a few months – valiantly joined the parade, chauffeuring me to his house which was a welcome change of scenery, for home-cooked, usually Italian dinners. At first he had to feed them to me, but once I could actually manage a fork with my non-dominant and somewhat less injured left-hand, he would meticulously cut up each meal into small bites. Talk about a trial by fire for a new relationship.

Another new experience was physical therapy. Once I finally got past the metal stabilizers, a moment I celebrated with a glass of champagne, by the way, rounds of physical therapy followed. Three times a week for what would be months I had to fight against the atrophy that had set in as I healed. Having been immobilized for so long, my arms needed to learn how to become useful again. Constant, repetitious exercises were the only way my wrists could learn how to bend and turn again and to find the strength to coax the muscles in my fingers into a reasonable grip. I had an amazing therapist who made the monotony of these sessions bearable, even enjoyable. Barb would distract me by asking me about my family and regaling me with funny anecdotes about her own, all the while pushing me to get stronger and more fluid in my wrist movements. And the warm wax massages she would confer upon my achy limbs at the start each round of therapy almost made me feel like I was at a spa. I just had to close my eyes and ears to shut out the buzzing fluorescent glow of hospital lighting.

The physical toll on my body from the bike accident was one thing. Healing sucks up a lot of energy. But then there was the much more practical aspect that my lengthy convalescence and recovery had on my work life. As a video producer and writer, I was used to making my living through my fingertips, as it were, with my computer being the backbone of my productivity. Now, suddenly, I had to ask my work colleagues to step into the middle of all of my ongoing projects and shepherd them to completion to my clients' satisfaction with very little assistance from me. It was a little like asking someone to build a house without the blueprints. Now. Today. Luckily, I had talented co-workers and understanding clients, not to mention super supportive bosses.

As the sole breadwinner of my family, the impact on me financially was also an issue. My sick leave carried me for a while, but when my rehabilitation stretched into weeks and then months, one of the owners of our small production company paid me a visit.

"We just can't afford to keep you on the payroll any longer," Rich explained. "We'll hold your job for you until you are able to come back, but our accountant says we just can't keep paying you indefinitely. I hope you understand."

I did understand. This decision was probably as tough on my bosses as it was on me. They were able to maintain my health insurance, at least, so that was a relief. And, luckily, I had some short-term disability insurance that kicked in to tide us over until I could return to work, nearly four months after the accident.

It was a truly humbling experience to find myself so completely incapacitated on so many levels but it was also, curiously, a kind of gift. Apparently, it took a momentous smack in the head for me to realize the magnitude of the love and generosity of spirit that encircled my life. My work, my friends, and relatives, my neighbors and even some distant acquaintances all rallied to my cause. Then, of course, there was my immediate family. I never questioned that my daughters loved me, but this was one tall order. With absolutely no use of my wrists, hands or arms, my ability to do even the simplest tasks was lost. Yet my girls brought more kindness, selflessness, and much-needed humor to the situation than I would ever have thought possible.

Who could imagine when or how it would be absolutely normal to brush Mom's teeth, shave her legs, give her a shower or even help her use the bathroom? Beyond the personal hygiene, there was the mere matter of running a large house, keeping it clean, mowing the lawn, doing the grocery shopping and paying the bills, not to mention the endless trips to the doctor and physical therapist. All of this came at no small cost to my kids. Kathleen voluntarily cut short a much-coveted year of post-graduate service work in Oregon to help nurse me back to wellness. Annie, at twenty-four, had a master's degree in progress and a career that demanded much of her time, yet she was always on deck. And Molly and Colleen between college studies, work, and busy social lives seemed to drop everything to make time for me. I was always told that the defining role of a parent is to give selflessly to your children. Never did I imagine that gift would be returned a thousandfold in all that my daughters did to heal my wrists, lift my spirits, and prove a devotion to me that was boundless.

Eight weeks after my bicycle accident I finally got the Frankenstein-like metal stabilizer bars removed from both of my arms. This was truly something to smile about.

CHAPTER SEVENTEEN

ONE STEP FORWARD...

"I can be changed by what happens to me, but
I refuse to be reduced by it."

Maya Angelou, American poet

Sometimes life felt like one of those weighted kids' punching bags that keeps popping back up in your face no matter how many times you try to beat it back, leering at you with that plastic, near-sinister smile. Between dealing with all my daughters' needs and issues absolutely by myself from the time they were near babies into adulthood, and then facing some significant out-of-the-blue health challenges myself, I always seemed to find that nagging self-doubt bouncing back in my face. Not every day. Not all the time. But there were days when I wondered if I would ever feel fully prepared to deal with life in all its intricacies, despite how far we, as a family, and I, personally, had come after losing Steve.

I still worried that my efforts to assume the role of two parents was falling short. Some days I wasn't even sure if I was doing an adequate job of being even one. As adults, my girls didn't know how to sew on a button or iron a shirt. They still came to me looking for the best way to cook asparagus, like I was some sort of culinary expert, or when they sought guidance in how to cast their first ballots once they hit age eighteen. And which Wisconsin teams were most worthy of their support? There were so many questions for which I felt ill equipped to provide an answer. There had been too many other demands on my time to even consider such trivialities.

I probably needed to cut myself some slack. After all, all of my daughters had graduated from high school, and gone on to college, and even post-graduate studies. For the most part, they seemed happy and well-adjusted with varying degrees of ambition driving them through life. My arms were on the mend after my terrible bike accident. And, with ten years of successful mammograms and regular follow up, cancer seemed almost a thing of the past. There was always a touch of trepidation until the radiologist's report came back clean each year, but overall my health was good.

And I was preparing for my third year of teaching in Italy of all places, under a new mantle. I had been asked to be the assistant director of the program. So, in addition to teaching multi-media journalism, I was now responsible for marketing this study-abroad opportunity and making sure our curriculum was relevant and interesting to potential students. I was honored by the trust my director placed in me and happy to take on the additional work, figuring it was well worth my while to squeeze it in between the duties of my regular full-time job and my demands at home. I loved the program, my teaching colleagues, and a country that was increasingly feeling like something of a second home. My Italian heritage bubbled proudly to the surface for five weeks every summer.

I felt I was making important strides in my professional life while still juggling my duties on the home front. There were a lot of evening meetings and phone calls with the Italy team to make the preparations for the upcoming trip. But luckily, my girls were older. Three of the four were living on their own and not needing or, quite frankly, wanting any daily input from Mom. So my devotion to the needs of the Italy program were not a drain on my daily responsibilities.

Or so I thought.

My third daughter, Molly had dropped out of the private university where her financial and emotional life had gone off the rails freshman year. Her repeated, uncontrolled, reckless spending had, unbeknownst to me, gotten her thousands of dollars in debt, debt that had nothing to do with school. When she took the tuition money I'd given her for that semester's bill and instead used it to quiet the debt collectors from the credit card companies, that was the final straw. In a decision that hurt me perhaps as much as it did her, I ended my commitment to pay her undergraduate tuition, a promise I had made to each of my daughters many years before. I saw no other recourse.

To her credit, Molly was determined to finish her degree even without my financial support. She enrolled in the local public university and reluctantly moved back home in order to afford it. The price was right even if it meant living with Mom. Intellectually, she knew she had no one to blame but herself for her huge financial predicament. Still, she seemed angry with me for not bailing her out. She barely communicated with me, and, at twenty, saw no reason to share any details of her personal life beyond answering the most basic inquiries from me. She resented any suggestions I would offer about getting outside help with her spending problem, and we danced around any talk of feelings. We were two entities operating in the same universe but in very separate orbits. It was a precarious arrangement at best.

It started in January and then became more noticeable despite the baggy sweatshirts and yoga pants that Molly insisted on wearing as her daily uniform. Molly was putting on weight. At first, I dismissed it. I tended to overeat when I was upset or angry. Perhaps she took after me in that one regard. But I felt I was in no position to suggest she eat better or try to get more exercise. My daughter was barely speaking to me as it was without opening up that can of worms. Yet as the pounds continued to add up, my worries did, too.

The thought did occur to me that one reason for weight gain could be pregnancy. Molly was pretty secretive about her social life but I had no inkling that there might be a boyfriend in the picture. Plus, she seemed to be kind of a homebody, only going out to her part-time job or school as far as I could tell. And given our walking-on-eggshells relationship at that time, there was no way I felt I could outright ask her, what? Are you pregnant or are you just getting fat? Talk about a lose/lose situation.

I even tried to do an end-around, to get some answers without having to blurt out what I increasingly worried might be Molly's new reality. On a long drive to visit relatives in Michigan that spring, it happened that Molly and I were alone together in the car for a good six hours. This was my chance to try to get my twenty-year-old to open up to me. She had no doors to shut in my face. No place to disappear to in order to avoid my questions. Again, afraid of a blatant confrontation I spoke of her upcoming birthday.

"You know, Molly," I said. "You're going to be twenty-one soon, officially a woman, you could say."

"Yeah," Molly agreed, non-committal.

"Have you got a gynecologist that you see? You really should be getting regular annual physicals now," I offered, hoping this little talk would ease open the door for Molly to tell me if she was pregnant. My lame, chicken-hearted attempt failed.

"I know, Mom. I'm on it," was all I got in response. It was clear Molly was not taking my bait.

I tried to tell myself that I'd given her ample opportunity to tell me if she was going to have a baby, and when I got nowhere, I convinced myself that I must have over-thought the situation. I busied myself with the many obligations before me. The Italian study-abroad program was just a few short weeks away, and it needed my attention. There were travel arrangements to be made for our contingent of faculty and two dozen students. I needed to create four weeks of lesson plans and help iron out the seemingly endless details of living and working abroad.

It was Mother's Day. My flight to Italy was on May 27th. Nineteen days away. That's when Molly dropped the bomb. She was pregnant. Not only that, but the baby was due in four weeks. I can't say I was totally surprised, although the timing threw me for a loop. An ostrich can only stick its head in the sand for so long before coming up for air.

Still, this was no splash of cold water to the face. It was more like the winning basketball team's ice water cooler dumped on the coach from behind. There was no time to process anything. The news was so overwhelming, the responsibilities so life-changing, and the days to answer a litany of questions were waning.

Tick. Tock.

What would she do with this child? I wanted Molly to at least consider that she had options, limited as those were well into her third trimester. Through a friend I hastily found a social worker who knew the ins and outs of adoption. She could at least walk Molly through what that might look like, to explain the concept of open adoptions. That turned out to be an exercise in futility. Molly listened politely to placate me, but in her heart of hearts she had already decided she would keep the baby, a boy.

Tick. Tock.

What about the child's father? Apparently, there were two possible candidates, neither of whom I knew, and neither was even in the picture any more. Molly was not interested in contacting either of them to let them know about their possible impending fatherhood. I thought she needed to consider that more deeply. This was an important decision that would affect her child for life. He had a right to know both of his parents, or at least know who they were. But in the face of my daughter's absolute refusal to budge on this issue, I resolved that would have to be a battle for later. There were too many more pressing issues that needed immediate attention.

Tick. Tock.

Where and how would she live with this new baby? My house was long past the nursery stage. There was no place for a newborn to sleep, or be bathed, or to try out his first apple sauce or pureed green beans. No changing table or diaper pails. Baby bottles, nipples, and Tommee Tippee cups had been purged long ago, along with any miniature spoons or plastic divider plates. We had no toys. No children's books. No stroller. No cuddly newborn blankets.

Tick. Tock.

And what about clothing this child? The few baby things I had stashed away from my own kids were mostly of the pink, ruffled, velvet variety, the kind of attire that made for darling holiday photos. Not exactly right in this moment. Molly's son needed onesies, sleepers, diapers, practical everyday things. And plenty of them.

Tick. Tock.

Tick. Tock.

Perhaps selfishly, my biggest questions, my biggest concerns, were for my daughter and the enormous consequences of this choice she was making. The prospects of this new life brought with it a sadness and fear for the future of my own baby, my Molly. I knew more than I ever dreamed I'd have to know about single parenting when it was thrust upon me. It was a hard road, energy-sucking and draining, both emotionally and financially. Molly had no idea the magnitude of what she was stepping into.

And what would happen to her dream of becoming a doctor? At just twenty years old, how could she possibly finish college or even think about medical school, internships or residency with a baby on her hip? She was already drowning in school loan debt. Her part-time waitressing job wasn't taking care of her living expenses as one person. How could she possibly afford child care, not to mention all the other costs of raising a child?

Those worries and countless more kept me awake at night, as my usual mom instinct kicked into high gear. I needed to fix this situation. Clearly I had no influence on Molly's decision to raise this child on her own, but, given that mandate, shouldn't I step in and somehow make it all better? Was I even capable of providing what she needed in this moment? This was no playground booboo you could fix with a band aid and a kiss. I found myself second-guessing my worthiness as a parent yet again. I must have done something wrong, or failed to do something right, for my daughter to end up at this momentous crossroads with her entire future on the line. One step forward, two steps back.

Then the full weight of my personal dilemma struck me. I was leaving the country in a matter of days and would be gone for five weeks. With the baby due in early June, the strong likelihood was that I wouldn't even be on the same side of the ocean when my first grandchild decided to arrive.

Who would be there to coach Molly with her breathing and hold her hand or provide her ice chips as she went through the scary, excruciating process of labor and delivery? And what about those first challenging days at home? Learning how to breastfeed when the baby just refused to latch on. Coping during those middle-of-the-night feedings when all you craved was someone to relieve you and give you just a few more moments of much-needed sleep. The tips for giving seven pounds of squirming, crying, slipperiness his first bath. I felt like I owed Molly the wisdom and experience that only a mother of four, her mother of four, could provide in this intensely personal moment.

I wondered if my going off to Italy was callous and insensitive, if I was abandoning my daughter at a crucial crossroads in her life. On the other hand, ditching out on my commitment to teach the study abroad program and also be its assistant director felt like another form of abandonment. I would be putting the university professor and friend who had hired me for the job, not to mention my other teaching colleagues, in a really bad spot on extremely short notice. Plus, selfishly, I really craved my Italy experience. It inspired me, and challenged me, and gave me new purpose. In nearly three years, it had become a personal devotion, an exciting sabbatical, a feather in my professional cap. I really didn't want to give it up.

As I found myself doing so often at critical junctures in my life, I sought the advice of my sisters, my daughters, and my dear friend, Kathy.

"You are not <u>not</u> getting on that plane," Kathy counseled. "Your Italy trip is a huge commitment. You've worked hard for it, and you owe it to yourself to go."

My sisters agreed. "I'm here in Milwaukee," Joan reminded me in her best big-sisterly way. "I will be here for Molly until you return. She and the baby will be fine."

Molly's sisters all chimed in, too. "We'll stay at the house, Mom. Molly won't be alone," Annie insisted. "And we've always got Aunt Joanie, Aunt Cindy and Aunt Julie to turn to if we have questions. You need to go. We've got this."

Annie even backed up her assurances to me with a phone call on the sly to the Italy program director's son, who was also part of the study abroad staff.

"I can remember calling Vince before you left, and just telling him what was happening, and being like 'make sure she's ok,'" Annie told me later. She didn't want me to feel guilty about going to Italy.

After considerable reflection, plenty of trepidation, and lots of prayers, I decided to go. And, as if to signal that I was doing the right thing, Miles Steven decided to make his appearance, pink and healthy, and sixteen days early, three days before I was to leave for Italy. I got my wish to be at my daughter's side as she gave birth and to even cut the cord for my beautiful grandson.

A few days later, I got on the plane bound for Rome, perhaps appreciating for the first time just how far I had come and how much our family had grown, after losing our husband and father. This complicated journey toward independence and resiliency had proven to be a gift. I finally had bested that clown punching bag. Even if it dared pop back in my face down the road, I was prepared. I had been able not just to survive all manner of hardships starting with Steve's death, but I had come to learn that I had earned the ability to move forward and thrive.

New mother Molly was just twenty when she became a
single mother to baby Miles, my first grandchild.

Chapter Eighteen

GIFTS

"You don't lose everything when someone dies. You do lose their physical presence, but their physical presence is not all of them, and it never was all of them even when they were alive. Spirit is very strong. Emotion is very strong. Their energy is very strong."

Bruce Springsteen, musician

It was a warm spring afternoon, early on in our young married life. Steve came home from work early, which was unusual, but even more curious was the unexpected gift he held out to me. It wasn't remotely close to my birthday, and even the nearest Hallmark holiday, Sweetest Day, was months away.

I opened the bag and not very eloquently or kindly exclaimed "What do you expect me to do with these?"

They were Brooks running shoes, with some clever name like Vantage, or something to that effect. And they were even in my size which was quite a feat for a guy who regularly mis-guessed my dress or sweater sizes by a mile, both too large and too small.

"They're running shoes," Steve patiently explained.

"I'm aware of what they are," I retorted. "But you are the runner, not me!"

"I thought it would be fun if we could run together," he said. "There are a lot of great parkways we could explore, and a lot of nice runs we could sign up for."

The words "nice" and "runs" were not ones I would have ever put together, but I thought it was sweet that Steve wanted to find something new to share with me. So I gamely laced up the shoes, switched into shorts and a t-shirt and decided to give it a try. I ran without stopping all the way...around the block...and thought I might die. My lungs were on fire. And I considered myself a fairly fit person. But stubborn determination and pride, coupled with Steve's not always so gentle prodding, turned me into a runner, or at least a decent jogger. Knowing that I worked best under the pressure of a deadline (I was a news reporter after all), I set my sights on a 5-mile race for the local children's hospital three months down the road. Each day that summer, Steve and I would add a few more blocks onto our running routes, building up for race day, and he gamely would circle back and catch up with me when I couldn't keep pace with him. I think he was nearly as determined as I to reach my goal.

When the big day came, I joined 17,000 other crazies pumped with adrenalin, running through downtown Milwaukee that Saturday morning. The first mile took us past the hospital that was the beneficiary of our efforts. It was inspiring and humbling to see dozens of kids in their hospital gowns shouting cheers of encouragement to us from their windows. Everyone was swept up in the moment. As our throng of runners made its way through east side neighborhoods awash in fall colors, other well-wishers lined the route, two and three people deep. They were clapping, cheering, and cooling us down with garden hoses while at the same time turning up the heat, encouraging the momentum, by blaring Tom Petty and Bruce Springsteen from their porches. I was hooked. Crossing that finish line along a glimmering Lake Michigan shoreline that September day was exhilarating, both physically and emotionally. It launched what would become a life-long allegiance.

Much as I enjoyed the physical benefits of staying in shape by running regularly, it wasn't until Steve died so unexpectedly that I truly appreciated the gift he had given me. Not that first pair of running shoes, but the positive impact that a good run would have on my psyche for years to come. Countless times in the days, weeks, and years after his death, I would hit the pavement during moments of despair or anxiety or worry, almost as if I was actually running away from home, and kids, and all the responsibilities in my life. Yet I always returned about an hour later and not solely out of my sense of duty. My running made me calmer and gave me a new resilience and a clearer head so that I could tackle whatever challenging situations still awaited me. Those benefits were probably there, hovering below the surface, even as Steve and I clocked miles together during his lifetime. I just didn't recognize the full value of that gift until he was gone.

It seems odd, even absurd to suggest that anything positive could result from the loss of someone so significant. Yet there are countless examples, countless gifts, that I discovered as a result of Steve's death. In many ways these gifts helped me endure the relentless responsibilities of single motherhood; helped me find the stamina to somehow balance a challenging job when I was dog-tired; helped bring me back from what I'm sure was the brink of depression when life just seemed too overwhelming.

One of those abiding gifts, a gift that is still carried by me and my daughters to this day, was Steve's love of family. Coming from a large family who suffered the loss of their own father when Steve was only seven, Steve had a particular devotion to and admiration for his mom, who raised her six children single-handedly. And he was close to his siblings, particularly his younger sister and brother. At Steve's funeral, little brother David recounted how generous Steve always was with him from an early age. He related a story from their youth. David was eight or nine years old and desperately wanted a new bike, but their widowed mother couldn't afford it.

"So Steve, who was five years older than me, took money from his paper route," David recalled. "He went and bought me a brand-new green Schwinn Stingray bike with a banana seat and it was pretty cool. As I look back, that was just Steve."

Steve liked the fact that I came from a big, close-knit family, too, with six siblings and a growing brood of young nieces and nephews, despite the one stumbling block that threatened to be a deal breaker, my mother. When they first met, my mom and Steve locked horns a lot, probably because their personalities were so much alike. Both were extremely strong-willed and determined that they were always right. My mom was convinced this brash, outspoken young man just wasn't good enough to marry her "Gaelbug." But when her pleading fell on deaf ears, Muzzie ultimately relented. She came to the wedding and over the years, she came to love him, and he her. In fact, my mother's funeral was one of the only times I ever saw Steve cry.

Certainly, Steve had clashes with many of his own family members at times, too. His outspoken nature often came at the cost of hurt feelings, and it took some maturing for him to learn the art of being tactful, of moving on, agreeing to disagree if necessary. He came to appreciate what might be lost if he didn't adopt this approach. Ultimately, nothing was more important than family to him or to me, and that was something we vowed to instill in our daughters.

Molly recognized that gift from her dad long after he was gone.

"We bounce back better, I feel, because when we have little dramas or fights or arguments within our family, we don't stay mad at each other for long," Molly said. "I feel like there is nothing that would ever come between us that we wouldn't be able to talk about, and get over, and move on in our relationships."

My other daughters have echoed that same sentiment, expressing frustration, particularly with extended family, when they choose to let petty disagreements or old wounds divide them from those we should hold most dear.

"How can you lose someone like we lost Dad," they've often told me, "and not appreciate that life is too short, that no argument is worth cutting off your family?"

Another gift that I received from Steve was one I may have appreciated to a certain extent while he was alive, but its value compounded exponentially after his death, helping me to become a stronger, more self-assured, and self-sufficient woman and mother. Steve was always one with a vision beyond the moment. He was much more willing than me to take some qualified risks in pursuit of a brighter future. I was prone to the cautious side, particularly when it came to our finances. It was Steve who convinced me to buy our family home. At the time, I couldn't imagine how the six-figure price tag was anything we could possibly afford in our young marriage with our first baby on the way. But Steve was sure it was a good investment in a neighborhood that we coveted and one that would slip through our fingers if we didn't act quickly. The bank obviously agreed, so in the span of four short weeks, despite my misgivings, we found, purchased, and moved into the home that would be the foundation of our family for decades to come. Of course, it helped that he was able to sweet talk the original owner of the home into a reduced five-figure price. At eighty-five and heading into a nursing home, she was delighted to pass on the legacy of brick and mortar that she and her husband had built to a new generation. And she seemed rather taken by the celebrity of the couple who would buy her home – the young alderman and his very pregnant, TV news reporter wife.

That willingness to weigh some well-researched risks against the benefits they might produce played out countless times in our marriage, and made a believer of me when it counted most. After Steve passed away, with the reasonable assurance of a family friend and advisor that we were financially sound, I dipped my toes into new ventures. I remodeled a bathroom, replaced my old car with a brand new mini-van, and, at my friend Kathy's urging, bought five plane tickets to Florida for Easter break. Splurging on a family vacation with Kathy and her girls turned out to be less crazy and more necessary than I appreciated at the time. Getting away from Wisconsin's bone-chilling winter for a week in the warm sunshine, just steps away from a sandy beach and an aqua-blue pool, was a revitalizing, relaxing, restorative retreat for me and my four little girls. It's a tradition I've carried on with my family in some form ever since. And to think, had Steve been alive, I might have argued against such an extravagance.

Steve's influence paid off in another important way when it came to choosing one of the most important aspects of responsible parenting, our kids' education. As a city employee, Steve was required to live in the city of Milwaukee, which was no hardship. We both loved our neighborhood and were proud to be part of an urban community that, while it had its challenges, also offered an exceptional park system, major league sports, great theatre, concerts and so much more. One drawback, however, was that, at the time, the city's public schools offered only a lottery system...a mere roll of the dice for getting our girls into a neighborhood school that they could walk to every day. The thought of packing our little girls, our babies, onto a bus every morning, for a trip across town that might be an hour's ride in each direction, scared the daylights out of me and was a total non-starter. The alternative was a parochial school. Just blocks from our house, it seemed a good fit for our young family. Plus, we liked the idea of having some element of religion in our kid's formal education.

The downside was that a private school comes at a cost, and multiplying that tuition out for eight years of elementary school times four children, was a huge financial commitment. In fact, when Steve died, one of my greatest worries, other than if I could afford to keep our house, was if I'd have to yank our kids out of the comforting cocoon of their school and the teachers, classmates, and sports teammates who had become so precious. After a long, hard look at my finances, I determined that with some belt-tightening, the girls could stay put through grade school. But then high school and college loomed on the horizon. More big decisions to be tackled, once again without the advice or, quite frankly, the income of a second parent.

By the time Annie hit eighth grade most of her classmates were already eyeing the all-girl parochial high school, Divine Savior Holy Angels, as the next step. The peer pressure for her to follow suit, both on her and on me, was enormous. I was torn. The tuition was nearly $6 thousand a year and that didn't count books, fees, uniforms, or any extracurriculars...a huge leap beyond grade school tuition which had been a stretch in and of itself. And it wasn't lost on me that whatever decision I made for Annie would have to be multiplied out times four, with the other girls right on her heels in school. As the dollar signs started to add up in my head, the free public high school was beginning to look more attractive.

Then Annie, who was determined to stay with her circle of best friends into high school, reminded me "Daddy always said I would go to DSHA."

It was true. Steve, who was not even Catholic, had been adamant that this Catholic, all-girls high school was the best choice for our daughters. He had been super impressed by our two nieces who had graduated from DSHA, certainly with strong academic credentials but, even more impressively, they exuded a sense of self-worth, confidence, and leadership. Unlike many seventeen-year-old girls, they knew exactly what they wanted to accomplish in life, and had a plan for how to get it, much to the credit of the education they had received.

I resolved to find a way. Swallowing my pride, I applied for financial aid, a rigorous application process that meant sharing the details of my tax returns, year after year, with the powers-that-be at the high school, admitting to perfect strangers that I couldn't manage DSHA without help. Annie, followed by her three sisters, all resigned themselves to doing their parts with work-study jobs at the school and a variety of part-time work outside of school. They applied for and received many small scholarships that helped us reach our goal year after year. It was a family commitment that we had to sign onto together, sending them to a school where the average family income was well beyond our own. I'm sure it wasn't easy for them to do their work-study jobs with the sometimes condescending attitudes of their wealthier peers, but they never complained, at least not to me. I like to think they received a good education on many levels, not the least of which was being self-sufficient. Perhaps that was another back-handed gift that resulted from losing their dad.

That self-sufficiency certainly came to fruition with Molly as she took on the role of single mother with a renewed sense of purpose. Miles' birth, to my mind, was the one thing that years of pleading, arguing, and heated debates could not produce. It transformed Molly into a committed, driven young woman, determined to create a good life for herself and her son, perhaps in some way modeling her recollection of the warm, loving example her own father had set for her.

Molly went on to graduate from a university with a renowned school of nursing. She became a registered nurse, found a good job working in labor and delivery, and became a strong, loving, and resourceful single mother.

"I think being raised by a single mom and not just a single mom, but a successful single mom," Molly would later tell me, "showed me that I could pretty much do whatever I wanted to do and that adversity doesn't need to stop you from achieving what you want in life."

Adversity as a gift. Who knew?

I was so honored when Kathleen chose to run her first marathon with me as her training partner. Steve's gift of running lives on.

Molly proudly sharing her nursing school graduation day with Miles, just one month shy of his fifth birthday.

Chapter Nineteen

LEGACY

"Your loved ones may have left this Earth but they never leave your heart. They will always be with you."

Joseph R. Biden, 46th US President

"I, Colleen Cullen, do solemnly swear that as a member of the Bar of this Court, I will support the Constitution of the United States and the Constitution of the State of Wisconsin."

As I sat in the marbled halls of the Wisconsin Supreme Court, a solid mahogany banister dictating where we spectators were and weren't allowed, tears of pride welled up in my eyes. I wasn't intending to get emotional, but then again, this was a big deal. My baby was formally admitted to the Bar. The event itself was relatively brief and not exactly riveting. One of the justices delivered remarks that seemed more focused on himself than on the candidates before him. Then the group stood up in unison and recited their oath. Yet for all that it wasn't, it was still the capstone on a long journey to reach this prestigious achievement.

Colleen's graduation from law school had been a much more festive occasion, a joy-filled weekend of ceremonies and parties in Washington, D.C., capped by a formal black-tie ball at the National Portrait Gallery. For all its pomp and circumstance and glitter though, there was still more work ahead. The much-dreaded Bar exam, an event that struck terror into the hearts of most law school grads, still stood between Colleen and her dream. So, after many additional months of intense self-study, the news finally arrived.

"I PASSED THE BAR!!!" A simple text message from Colleen to me conveyed both joy and enormous relief. My youngest daughter was now an attorney. What a long and winding road it had been.

I must have had a sense that Colleen probably wouldn't remember her crazy, loving Daddy, having had only three short years to spend with him. A few months after Steve was snatched from our lives, I remember writing to him in my journal. "If Colleen ever claims she doesn't remember you, I hope she'll read this and see that's not true," I wrote. "We had your *Kids' Tape '95* on in the car today – it's become a staple in our diet of music to drive to – and the Box Tops' 1967 hit "The Letter" came on. Colleen pipes up, out of nowhere, 'this is one of Daddy's favorite songs!'"

When I think of the lovingly-chosen selections on that tape, made for what would become our last family vacation to northern Wisconsin, I can't help thinking of the legacy Steve left for all of us. With the passage of time, the memories don't rise to the surface nearly as often as they did when we were all in the throes of unspeakable grief. Yet, in ways both obvious and subtle, almost subconscious, Steve has put a lasting imprint on our hearts, our lives.

Certainly, music is one part of that legacy. Years of bedtime songs that included "Lemon Tree," "Where Have All the Flowers Gone," and more than an occasional Beatles' tune, have long since become staples in the musical diets not just of my kids, but of my kids' kids. To hear one of my grandsons belting out every lyric of Bruce Springsteen's "Thunder Road" while his three-year-old sister dances along and even the one-year-old baby rocks in a fit of giggles to the tune, makes my heart almost burst with joy, and delight, and wonderful memories. Their mother, Annie, has a simple explanation – music was on the stereo in our house all the time she was growing up and it's a tradition she continues, though now on her phone, thanks to Spotify and Pandora.

"I don't know if I'd like any of the music that I like without Dad," she recalls. "Because so much of what I still like is the old school stuff, Billy Joel and Tom Petty, even Peter, Paul and Mary!"

Colleen's evolution since Steve's death is another example of his legacy, one that particularly touches me and helps me realize that his life's experience lives on. Here was a kid, only three when her dad died, who finally, as a teenager, reluctantly admitted to herself and to me that she really had no memories of him. Crushing as this was to hear, although I'd long suspected it was true, I had to smile at how present Steve, a Milwaukee Common Council leader for years, was in her life and in her aspirations for the future.

Steve had graduated from the University of Wisconsin-Milwaukee with a degree in political science. Colleen did that, too, but she didn't just study politics, she lived it. On campus she almost single-handedly resurrected a dormant College Democrats organization, bringing it back to a vibrant, active life. Her work was so well received that she ultimately rose to a leadership role on a statewide level, organizing political conventions and achieving a first-name standing with many of the state's elected leaders and more than one member of Congress.

It was that activism and commitment to social justice, coupled with outstanding grades, that helped propel her to law school. The day that she was admitted to Georgetown University, one of the top-ranked law schools in the country, I could sense that her dad and his influences were coursing through her veins. She didn't consciously set out to follow in his footsteps. She might not remember him. But there's no doubt he was working within her.

To this day she remains an active and firm believer in our political system, in the value of community and of social justice. She put her prestigious law degree to work not in a high-powered law firm that such a degree could command, but in public service, defending the rights of people accused of crimes who cannot afford an attorney. The example set by her father based solely on borrowed memories and perhaps, I like to think, a bit of DNA, clearly helped shape her development.

"I know that as early as second grade, I was interested in becoming mayor and that I was interested in politics," Colleen says.

By the third grade, she was going toe-to-toe with any of her classmates willing to debate local politics.

"I was having arguments with anyone who would listen to me and that didn't stop until, ever," she laughingly remembers. "So I can't really point to where that came from besides what people tell me about Dad's personality."

There is so much evidence of Steve's thumbprints on all of our lives. One in particular has taken on a life of its own, far greater than any of us would have imagined. Several of my girls have become runners over the years, mostly recreational, but not all. Kathleen has completed a couple of marathons, including Boston, a feat that had to have roots in that long-ago inspiration Steve once gave me to pick up the sport. That particular legacy, coupled with an ingrained predisposition to helping others plus a keen desire to keep Steve alive in our hearts, resulted in what would become an annual community event.

It was Steve's first birthday after he died, January 5, 1996. Steve's younger brother, David, suggested that some close friends and family go on a run through our neighborhood as a way of marking this important, yet heartbreaking day. That first year, there were maybe a dozen of us braving Wisconsin's cold to clock a couple of miles in Steve's memory. David suggested we should make this birthday run a tradition, inviting more people to join us each year, giving any money we raised from participation fees or donations to an appropriate cause, heart research and education.

So 1997 became the first official year of the Steve Cullen Healthy Heart Club Run/Walk (apologies to the Beatles' "Sgt. Pepper" album, a favorite of Steve's). We charted a five-mile running course and a two-mile walking path through a nearby park, got a local running club to help us track everyone's time, and then crossed our fingers. I was hoping we'd get a few dozen crazies to join us outdoors on a chilly twenty-six-degree morning, made even more brutal by winds of nineteen miles per hour, all in the name of a good cause. I was wrong. One hundred sixty-two folks came out and ran or walked in Steve's memory. What a thrill.

Since that first organized event, the run/walk has grown exponentially in size and reputation. More than two decades later, we regularly draw a crowd of five to six hundred participants and we've managed to raise more than a half-million dollars for heart research. There is now a specific scholarship that we fund in Steve's name, giving money to a promising young scientist doing research on heart disease. And the torch is being passed to a new generation, my daughters, who are proud of this tribute to Steve, to his legacy, and are working to keep the event going.

Annie remembers being a little embarrassed by the run at first, in those adolescent years when it was paramount to look cool to your classmates. She didn't like how the run posters and flyers we would put up at her school would again single her out as the student whose dad had died suddenly.

"I just can remember feeling weird about it as a kid," she explained. "It was bringing attention on our family again."

But the realization that the run was not going away, combined with years of maturity, helped Annie come to embrace the run/walk, even taking on a leadership role in organizing it each year. She was also the driving force behind getting the scholarship dedicated to her father's name, acting on the advice of doctors she knew through her work who insisted there should be a fitting tribute named for him for all the research his run supported.

"We want to do whatever we can to help other people hopefully avoid some of this in their lives, and it's one way that we still carry on Dad's legacy," Annie says.

That, and it's an opportunity to introduce Grandpa Steve to her own kids.

"My kids love it," Annie says. "So, I think for them having never met him, it's great to have that. It's a talking point every year about Dad."

Having grown up with it so much a part of their lives, all of my daughters look forward to this tribute to their dad and its impact on the community.

"I'm super proud of the run," Molly tells me. "It benefits so many other people, and the fact that you took that on right after Dad died is really impressive to me. You have shown us that you can use the bad things that have happened to you to make things better in the world."

January 5, 1996 was the unofficial start of the Steve Cullen Healthy Heart Run/Walk. Steve's brother and sister (on either side of me in the middle), encouraged a couple of friends and a few of our kids to run through our neighborhood in honor of Steve's birthday.

Long a highly-publicized and well-organized event, the Steve Cullen Run/Walk now attracts hundreds of participants every year, with all proceeds going to heart research and education.

CHAPTER TWENTY

EVOLUTION

"There are uses to adversity, and they don't reveal themselves until tested. Difficulty can tap unexpected strengths."

Sonia Sotomayor, US Supreme Court Justice

Perspective is a beautiful thing. In the immediacy of loss and grief, it's almost impossible to draw your next breath at times, the weight of the burden under which you are living is so overwhelming. Yet time gifts us with healing and discovery... and perspective.

I am looking around my increasingly crowded dining room table, quietly basking in the glow of the family gathering that surrounds me. It's been more than twenty-three years since Steve died. My girls, now ranging from their mid-twenties to their early-thirties, are all well into their careers. Three are married and my youngest is engaged.

It is Miles' eighth birthday, and my surprise first grandchild is now the elder statesman of the next generation of our family, joined by two other grandsons, my first granddaughter and three more grandbabies soon to join their ranks.

Somehow, miraculously, despite intervening adventures in South Africa, Washington D.C., Oregon, New Orleans, Italy and China, all of my daughters returned to Wisconsin and settled close to home, much to my surprise and great delight. I had always thought if one or two ended up nearby I would consider myself lucky and would happily travel to those who might land farther away. And yet, here they all were, regular participants in what had become an accidental tradition, weekly Sunday night dinners at Mom's. (Truly an accident, as anyone who knows my rather ordinary cooking could attest. It is no culinary expertise that draws them in week after week.)

As Miles blows out the candles on his cake, he makes a wish for whatever intrigue sits in an eight-year-old's heart. Simultaneously I offer my own silent wish, a prayer really, that we all continue to cherish these times together. It's not easy sometimes when the kids start fighting over a game or some of their parents get overly-aggressive defending their favorite sports' teams. Our dinners are often loud and messy. But they are still a treasure. We are together.

The bond we share as a family is certainly not exclusive, but I'm convinced that conquering this long and complicated journey of grief has brought us and kept us together in ways that not everyone is lucky enough to experience. It's a family dynamic that is not lost on my daughters.

"As we continue to grow and our families continue to get bigger and bigger, we still make time for all of us to be together every week, every single Sunday," Molly says. "No one I know does that. And that will have a huge impact on Miles as he gets older because his bond with his Gigi is way different. I never had a bond like that with our grandma. As he gets older Miles is going to realize 'wow,' how lucky he is to have such a tight family."

Colleen, too, sees a gift in the trauma associated with losing her dad. "It has made us way, way, way, closer than the average family, a cool outcome of a shitty situation," she explains. "I think we're just definitely more intertwined than the average family, for better or for worse, probably because of the fear of losing each other."

"It's weird to think that that's my normal, a life without a dad," Annie adds. "As a result, I think we have really high highs and really low lows, but we also have so many things in the middle that are so good. We're a lot closer than a lot of other families."

Kathleen's take is a bit broader in scope, not surprising coming from my "save the world" social worker daughter. "Losing Dad is really tragic and it changed the trajectory of my life," Kathleen says. "Not that it made it all better, but even when I would think 'oh this really sucks' it would help snap me out of that and realize there are a lot of kids who grow up without dads for different reasons, but I still have a mom who is loving, and motivated, and smart, and successful. Seeing others who don't have that has really helped me change my perspective."

How odd it is for me to hear my daughters express gratitude for the unwelcome reality of being raised by a single mother. They didn't ask for that, and I certainly would never have chosen this path. That is particularly gratifying coming from Molly, who made the scary choice to raise her newborn son on her own and then, despite tremendous odds, went on to finish college and earn her master's degree with minimal financial help from me.

"I could have easily not gone back to school and worked dead-end jobs and did whatever I needed to do in order to raise Miles, but I always knew that I could do more,"

Molly tells me. "You showed me that I could pretty much do whatever I wanted to do and that adversity doesn't need to stop you from achieving what you want in life."

And what a blessing it is to see that somehow this gift of overcoming adversity, achieving resiliency, and owning our shared grief may have seeped into the next generation. My second oldest grandson, Cullen, was in second grade when the coronavirus pandemic hit in 2020. That spring would have continued a years-long family ritual of spending Easter vacation in Florida with me, his Gigi, were it not for the country swallowing into itself worried about this deadly virus.

Cullen called me one warm April afternoon during his Easter break from school and invited me to go on a walk with him around the neighborhood. He wanted to relieve the tedium of being cooped up in the house. In between discussions of Minecraft exploits and the newest Lego Jumanji set he had received, there was a small lull in the conversation.

"You know, today would normally have been a sad day for us," I pointed out.

"Why is that, Gigi?," Cullen wanted to know.

I reminded him that on this day, if not for the pandemic, we would have been in Florida probably walking on the beach rather than through his neighborhood.

"Today would have marked the last day of our vacation," I told him. "We would have been so sad to be leaving the sun and surf for another whole year."

After a bit of thoughtful reflection, Cullen said something that completely threw me.

"Gigi," he said. "You know, I don't think this virus is all that bad."

Puzzled, I asked him to explain. Then, from my seven-year-old grandson came this.

"I think the virus has brought all of us closer together," Cullen told me.

My wise young grandson, while acknowledging that something was lost in this COVID time, was still able to look beyond, to appreciate what had been gained during the pandemic, the forced togetherness that, while sometimes irritating, also required us to take the time to look for the positive in the situation.

"I think the virus has brought all of us closer together."

I don't know if perspective is genetic, or if it is borne of growing up in a family where it has been hard won, but that spirit of resilience persists. It has made the process of owning grief achievable and, in many ways, a gift.

A 2019 family vacation included a new generation. Steve's legacy in the flesh!

ACKNOWLEDGEMENTS

To my content editors and devoted friends Joan Boyce and Mike Williams without whose continual encouragement and counsel this memoir would never have come into being.

To all of my sisters, extended family, and countless friends, especially Pat Muldowney, Kathy Bottoni, and Bill Thorn who have walked this challenging, frustrating, and rewarding path alongside me. Their insights and counsel helped me realize that out of unspeakable loss can come life-changing gifts we never would have imagined.

To the many, too numerous to mention, who have offered steadfast support throughout the writing and publication of this memoir. My particular thanks go to Larry Baldassaro, Megan Shikora Catana, Megan Sheehan, Paul Salsini, Natalie Sanchez, Liam Callanan, and my four daughters.

SOURCES OF EPIGRAPHS

Chapter One

"On the other side of a storm is the strength that comes from having navigated through it. Raise your sail and begin."

Williams, Gregory S. https://moderntherapy.online/blog-2/
2019/2/26/10-quotes-on-resilience.

Chapter Two

"Your story is what you have, what you will always have. It is something to own."

Obama, Michelle. *Becoming.* (New York, NY: Crown
Publishing, November 13, 2018).

Chapter Three

"Grief is the price we pay for love."

Honeyman, Gail. *Eleanor Oliphant is Completely Fine.* (New
York, NY: Pamela Dorman Books, May 9, 2017).

Chapter Four

Muteness. A state of refusing to speak, being unable to speak, or silence.

Vocabulary.com. https://www.vocabulary.com/dictionary/ muteness.

Chapter Five

"The loneliest moment in someone's life is when they are watching their whole world fall apart, and all they can do is stare blankly."

Fitzgerald, F. Scott. *The Great Gatsby.* (New York, NY: Charles Scribner's Sons, 1925).

Chapter Six

"Life is about not knowing, having to change, taking the moment and making the best of it, without knowing what's going to happen next."

Radner, Gilda. *Gilda Radner Quotes.* (n.d.). BrainyQuote.com. Retrieved May 19, 2022, from BrainyQuote.com Web site: https://www.brainyquote.com/quotes/gilda_radner_ 135101.

Chapter Seven

"I learned that courage was not about the absence of fear, but the triumph over it."

Mandela, Nelson. *15 Nelson Mandela Quotes.* Encyclopedia Britannica, https://www.britannica.com/list/nelson-mandela-quotes. Accessed 19 May 2022.

Chapter Eight

"We did not feel prepared to be the heirs of such a terrifying hour. But within it we found the power to author a new chapter, to offer hope and laughter to ourselves."

Gorman Amanda. *"The Hill We Climb."* *Poetry.com.* STANDS4 LLC, 2022. Web. 19 May 2022. https://www.poetry.com/poem/60572/the-hill-we-climb.

Chapter Ten

"Anger is a symptom, a way of cloaking and expressing feelings too awful to experience directly – hurt, bitterness, grief and, most of all, fear."

Rivers, Joan. https://www.quotemaster.org/q7793a11062927 f1e5a93624bdbcb5061

Chapter Eleven

"I struggle with weakness, shortcomings and inadequacies, and yet I resist asking for help. Please teach me to humble myself and cultivate the practice of seeking help from others."

Shriver, Maria. *I've been Thinking.* (New York, NY: Pamela Dorman Books, December 31, 2018).

Chapter Thirteen

"What lies behind you and what lies in front of you pales in comparison to what lies inside of you."

Emerson, Ralph Waldo. Source unknown.

Chapter Fourteen

"So before I save someone else, I've got to save myself."

Sheeran, Ed. "Save Myself." ÷ *Album*. Atlantic Records UK, 2017.

Chapter Fifteen

"If you don't see that growth is possible, you're not going to find it."

Sandberg, Sheryl. *Option B: Facing Adversity, Building Resilience, and Finding Joy.* (London: Random House UK, April 24, 2019).

Chapter Sixteen

"Sometimes life throws us a curve ball. It doesn't go the way we planned. All that matters is how we handle it and the person we become on the other side."

Halle, Karina. *Before I Ever Met You.* (Vancouver, British Columbia, Canada: Metal Blonde Books April 24, 2017).

Chapter Seventeen

"I can be changed by what happens to me, but I refuse to be reduced by it."

Angelou, Maya. Twitter Web App Mar 28, 2020, 8:10pm.

Chapter Eighteen

"You don't lose everything when someone dies. You do lose their physical presence, but their physical presence is not all of them, and it never was all of them even when they were alive. Spirit is very strong. Emotion is very strong. Their energy is very strong."

Love, Robert. *"Exclusive Interview with Bruce Springsteen on Love, Loss, Aging and New Album 'Letter To You.'"* AARP The Magazine, Oct/Nov 2020, September 24, 2020, p.38.

Chapter Nineteen

"Your loved ones may have left this Earth but they never leave your heart. They will always be with you."

Biden, Joseph R. Address Accepting the Democratic Presidential Nomination in Wilmington, Delaware Online by Gerhard Peters and John T. Woolley, The American Presidency Project https://www.presidency.ucsb.edu/node/342190, August 20, 2020.

Chapter Twenty

"There are uses to adversity, and they don't reveal themselves until tested. Difficulty can tap unexpected strengths."

Sotomayor, Sonia. (n.d.). AZQuotes.com. Retrieved May 19, 2022, from AZQuotes.com Web site: https://www.azquotes.com/quote/278283.

READERS' GUIDE FOR GROUP DISCUSSION

You may have noticed that my memoir does not follow a chronological timeline. That is intentional. Grief is not a linear process that you move through step by step to some appointed conclusion. You may think you've moved beyond a certain memory, or emotion, or challenge in your grief journey, only to have it overwhelm you again at some point or points down the road.

For that reason, I categorized my chapters largely by state of mind. I hope you will find this helpful as you discuss the book, reflecting on gifts you may have received in losing someone special in your own life.

Gael Garbarino Cullen

1. Talk about the effectiveness of the use of an "in your face" minute-by-minute time frame at the start of the book. What did you think was the most compelling minute. Why?
2. We learned about the early days of my marriage to Steve in chapter two. Was this important to set the tenor for the memoir? Why?

3. In planning the funeral of my husband, I encountered some unexpected obstacles but also many positive experiences. Have you ever benefited from a "spiritual hug" in a time of need?

4. Do you sometimes find yourself "word inadequate" at a funeral, as I describe in chapter four? Why is it so difficult for us humans to console one another when someone dies?

5. In chapter five, I talk about confronting the "beast of loneliness." How have you dealt with loneliness in your life?

6. Several times I shared an uncertainty about my future and my abilities as a single mother. In particular, in chapter seven, I discussed the nagging fear that, on my own, I might not be able to offer my girls a successful marriage role model. Do you agree with this idea or not? Why?

7. Depression and anxiety were critical emotional states discussed in "Owning Grief." Have you ever dealt with feeling "down" or anxious to the point where it felt paralyzing? What did you do about it?

8. In chapter ten, I focus on anger. Have you ever been "set off" by a seemingly insignificant event? What works best for you to defuse your anger?

9. At first, accepting help from others after Steve died challenged my resolve that I could "do it all." Have you ever found it difficult to accept help when you most need it? Do you ever reach out to help others in similar circumstances?

10. Chapter twelve describes the ups and downs of re-entering the dating world after losing my young husband. Have you ever found yourself in a similar situation after

a death or divorce? How did you handle it? Did your kids or others surprise you in their reactions?

11. Family traditions often had to change or evolve in Steve's absence. With each new "first," (first birthday, first Thanksgiving, first kid's dance recital, etc.) I had to brace myself for the moment, and, often, change the ritual to handle it. Have you ever experienced this? How did you react?

12. My diagnosis of cancer just six years after losing Steve felt like some higher power was, to coin a football term, "piling on." Have you ever had to deal with a serious health issue? Who or what helped you through it?

13. In chapter fifteen I talk about post-traumatic growth, perhaps best exemplified by my accepting an opportunity to teach overseas. Share a time when you took a bold new step that turned out well even if you had doubts about it at the time.

14. Have you or a loved one ever experienced a serious illness or accident, such as my crippling bike accident? What were the limitations or unexpected joys you or the person experienced as a result?

15. In chapter seventeen I found myself making a hard decision to put myself and my needs first. Have you ever encountered such a dilemma in your own life? What was that like for you?

16. After you have read chapter eighteen, can you relate to how a specific adversity ultimately made you stronger? Did you see it as a gift or not?

17. If you could ask the author one question what would it be? What might you want to know more or less about?

18. As a writer, what was the author's strongest talent? Consider, the tool of creating suspense, the minute by minute accounting of some events, the use of dialog and first person quotes, or something else.

19. Looking back at the quotes that opened each chapter, which one stood out to you or "spoke" to you the most? Why?

ABOUT THE AUTHOR

Gael Garbarino Cullen is an accomplished writer and video producer as well as a longtime TV and radio news reporter who covered everything from presidential politics to World Series baseball during her career. She loves rock and roll music and is an avid Detroit Tiger baseball fan, a nod to her hometown roots. She's passionate about running, not too far or too fast, although she has managed to muscle through two marathons.

She lives and works in Milwaukee, Wisconsin, where she is lucky enough to share time with her four daughters and their families, including a growing cache of grandchildren.

owninggrief.com